STRENGTH T[...]G
for Total Health and Wellness

Matthew Wagner | Gary Oden
Sam Houston State

Tim Sebesta | Ronnie Nespeca
Lone Star CyFair

Kendall Hunt
publishing company

Photos on pages 72, 73, 74, 76, 77, 78, 79, 81, 84, 86, 88, 92, 94, 95, 96, 97, 99, 100, 101, and 103 are from *Fundamentals of Weight Training* by Matthew C. Wagner, William E. Nix, and Gary L. Oden. Copyright © 2011 by Kendall Hunt Publishing Company. Reprinted by permission.

Cover image © Shutterstock, Inc.

www.kendallhunt.com
Send all inquiries to:
4050 Westmark Drive
Dubuque, IA 52004-1840

Copyright © 2013 by Kendall Hunt Publishing Company

ISBN 978-1-4652-1818-6

Printed in the United States of America
10 9 8 7 6 5 4 3 2 1

CONTENTS

Chapter 4

Developing a Strength Training Program   **27**

Chapter 10

Strength Training for Life

Chapter 11

INTRODUCTION TO STRENGTH TRAINING

INTRODUCTION

Weight training, strength training, or resistance training can and should be a lifelong activity for all males and females. The benefits of a continuous exercise program involving resistance exercise are numerous, and can be experienced by individuals of all ages. Combined with a comprehensive cardiovascular exercise program, flexibility training, and a proper nutritional intake, individuals can experience many fitness- and health-related benefits. These benefits include increased muscle mass, decreased fat tissue, decreased risk of heart disease, increased range of motion, decreased risk of injury, sport improvement, and even increased self-esteem! The perceptions of developing large, bulky muscles from lifting weights, the necessity of exercising for long duration with large resistance, or becoming "muscle bound" and losing flexibility are decades-old myths that have kept many individuals from participating in this program. However, these myths have been refuted in the research, and a proper resistance exercise program will have many more benefits than disadvantages! A comprehensive weight training program can begin at a young age and continue until old age, continuing to provide benefits and enjoyment through the life span.

Benefits of Resistance Exercise

Fitness is often described as a combination of five elements: cardiovascular conditioning, muscle strength, muscle endurance, flexibility, and body composition. A proper strength training program can have a positive effect on all of these different elements of fitness. By engaging in a circuit-type training routine and maintaining an increased heart rate throughout the circuit, strength training can positively impact the cardiovascular system (Pollock et al., 2000). A well-designed program regulating the amount of sets and repetitions can cause increases in muscle strength and muscle endurance. By working each repetition throughout the entire range of motion of the joint, weight training can cause a significant increase in a person's flexibility and range of motion. Finally, because muscle is metabolically active tissue, a well-balanced weight training program can cause dramatic decreases in body fat. Muscle utilizes anywhere from 6–35 calories per pound per day; therefore, by increasing muscle mass one can also experience a decrease in body fat percentage (Braith & Stewart, 2006). One additional benefit that has long term implications is the reduction of loss of bone mass with exercise. Weight training has been shown to increase bone mass density in all age groups, thereby reducing an individual's risk of osteoporosis in later years (Kohrt, Bloomfield, Little, Nelson & Yingling, 2004). Possibly one of the most important benefits of resistance exercise is the ability to improve an individual's quality of life. Everyday tasks such as performing household chores, or even lifting and carrying children and grandchildren are made easier to perform with resistance exercise. Also, the ability to begin and adequately sustain physical activity is one of the most positive benefits of a comprehensive strength and conditioning program.

Scenario:

You are asked to assist with improving the strength and health of a relative who has never exercised before. How can you convince him/her to engage in resistance exercise?

HISTORY OF WEIGHT TRAINING

The basic concept of overloading the human muscular system was the foundation of the beginning of resistance exercise. For example, historians report that over 3000 years ago Milo of Croton lifted a calf each and every day, thereby introducing the concept of progressive resistance with the overload principle. Probably Milo supplemented his training program with a form of progressive resistance, as certainly that this particular type of lift would stimulate only certain muscle groups. As the animal grew in size, so did the load on Milo's muscles, thereby increasing the workload.

In the Chou dynasty (1122–249 BC), Chinese soldiers were required to perform a strength test in order to get into the army. This involved pulling a bow with up to 90 pounds of resistance (Selby, 1997). The Romans experimented with weight training, as reported by Roman poets such as Martial. Certainly the Roman army was

© Shutterstock, Inc.

widely feared and respected, possibly in part due to their resistance training regimen. Weight training became a part of the curriculum in Europe when several universities in France and Germany offered weight training classes along with weight training books. The 1500s during the Renaissance was the next significant historical milestone in resistance exercise.

In the Greek era, individuals trained in an area utilizing weights called halteres, the predecessor of the modern dumbbell. The earliest version of the modern dumbbell took place in the 16th century. Because ringing a church bell was a difficult task, beginning ringers would train by swimming a rope lodged inside a bell. The rope made no sound; therefore it was "dumb." Another version of this definition was said to occur in the 1700s when a rod was placed between two church bells and the clapper was removed, thereby rendering them "dumb." Whichever version accounted for the definition, it is obvious that the beginning of formal resistance exercise began many years ago.

British military police stationed in India borrowed an idea from their Indian counterparts by swinging wooded clubs in order to increase their strength. This was incorporated into the British military training. In the late 19th century a Swedish physician named Gustav Zander built custom-made resistance exercise machines. These machines were remarkably similar to the current latissimus pull down machine as well as other different exercise apparatus. In 1876, Zander traveled to the United States to display his machines in Philadelphia, and American businesses purchased the machines for their spas around the country.

During the early part of the 20th century the concept of adding removable weights to the bars in order to increase and decrease resistance was developed. The concept of adding weights to different machines was also developed in this century.

Certain individuals have had tremendous influence on resistance exercise in the 20th century. Charles Atlas, Jack LaLanne, Bill Pearl, Joe Weider, and Arthur Jones all offered significant contributions to the growth and development of resistance exercise, weight training, and bodybuilding. These individuals helped form the foundation leading to the increased popularity of resistance exercise today.

Charles Atlas was born in in Italy in 1893 and came to Ellis Island in 1903. His original name was Angelo Sicilliano. Angelo began his workout program early when he was frequently picked on by bullies, and (as legend has it) a lifeguard allegedly kicked in the face of his 97-pound body. That was apparently a defining moment in Atlas's career. He determined that utilizing isometric opposition and adding range of motion to his muscles caused increased muscular hypertrophy. His concept of Dynamic Tension was met with skepticism by others who did not believe that significant hypertrophy could occur based on that principle alone. One of his friends saw his new physique and commented that he looked like the statue of Atlas on the top of the Atlas Hotel. The name stuck with him, and he added Charles to his nickname of Charlie. Atlas became a model for public sculptures, and his legacy lives on through the transformation of a "97-pound weakling into a real Man." Atlas has been called the Father of Modern Day Bodybuilding and Fitness.

While Atlas may have been referred to as the Father of Fitness, Jack LaLanne is often referred to as the Godfather of Fitness. Born in 1914 in California, LaLanne discovered early on the benefits of utilizing resistance exercise, and the positive effect it had on the body. Doctors at that time opposed weight training, as conventional wisdom implied that it caused heart attacks. LaLanne is credited with developing the first Smith machine, a revolutionary concept that allowed free weight movements in an entirely vertical movement pattern. He also helped develop the first leg extension, and other machines still utilized today in most gyms. He may be best known for his 1950s television fitness program, encouraging many to begin and continue their exercise programs. His overall contributions to fitness and strength training have revolutionized how fitness gyms operate today. LaLanne was the epitome of practicing what you preach, and maintained a strict exercise regimen throughout his life.

Bill Pearl was born in Oregon in 1930 and began his weight training career early in life, reportedly to defend himself from his older brother. He is a five-time Mr. Universe, winning his first bodybuilding title in 1953. Pearl's contributions to the sport of bodybuilding are numerous, including both individual competitions and coaching. He has run gyms in the Sacramento and Los Angeles areas for over 30 years, and has coached many major bodybuilding contest winners throughout his career. He continues his legendary workouts even today.

Joe Weider was born in Canada in 1919 and also learned the value of resistance exercise at an early age. His desire to work out and inspire others to do the same led to his publication of *Your Physique* in 1940. This magazine was successful and helped with the creation of other magazines including *Muscle and Fitness, Shape, Flex*, and others. Weider also started the Weider Barbell Company, offering weight sets and other exercise equipment by mail. He is credited with creating the Mr. Olympia contest, one of the premiere contests in bodybuilding. He also founded the International Federation of Bodybuilders (IFBB). Weider also is credited with developing the Weider Principles, developing and outlining ideas and concepts utilized by many of the best weight lifters and bodybuilders in the world. Weider was an avid exerciser until his death in 2013 at the age of 93.

Arthur Jones was born in Arkansas in 1926. Jones pioneered progressive and equal resistance with his development of the Nautilus machine. In the early 1970s he found that by utilizing a kidney-shaped device known as a cam, the resistance could be altered to match the strength curve of the muscle. The Nautilus machine was perceived as a logical barbell, as it took several of the detriments of free-weight training and offered a more efficient and potentially safer workout program. Jones pioneered the concept of High Intensity Training (HIT), preferring single sets performed until momentary muscular failure versus multiple sets at a lower intensity. His machines were integral in the strength development of professional football teams in the early 1970s, and continue to be utilized by sports teams and fitness centers today.

These individuals and many others have worked to shape our introduction into modern weight training and its benefits. Undoubtedly future individuals will pioneer new revolutionary concepts that will aid in the strength development of all individuals, athletes and non-athletes alike.

While females had engaged in weight training to some extent early on, women were more widely influence to begin resistance exercise around the 1980s and 1990s. While aerobics and group exercise classes were gaining in popularity, so was the concept that resistance training would enhance a women's physique, not detract from it. Programs such as Body for Life and others were influential in persuading women to get increasingly involved in resistance exercise.

Because of the increased popularity of exercise, many different manufacturing companies have been formed to handle this demand. Today there are hundreds of different equipment brands, and the exercise equipment market has branched out into many different areas. From computer-generated programs to compact exercise machines built for the traveling individual, exercise equipment has progressed significantly from just a rope inside a bell!

In the modern era of functional training, concepts like balance, core strength and core stability, agility, and others are of vital importance to athletes and non-athletes alike. Future generations will be shaped by forward-thinking individuals, strength machines, and training techniques that will work together in order to develop a stronger, quicker, and physically more impressive athlete.

PLANNING AN EFFECTIVE WEIGHT TRAINING ROUTINE AND MODALITIES

STEPS TO AN EFFECTIVE PROGRAM

Establish Goals

The first step in any program is to determine exactly what objectives you wish to accomplish. Goal setting is of primary importance, as this establishes the framework for the entire program. Regardless if you are seeking to improve athletic performance, working out to improve health status, or exercising to gain increased muscle mass, an accurate assessment of individual objectives should be initially performed. These goals should be measurable, concrete, and objective. "Getting in shape" is an abstract goal. To a bodybuilder, "in shape" may mean achieving 22-inch biceps, while to an 83-year-old woman, "in shape" may have more to do with maintaining everyday lifestyle activities. It is important that all goals and objectives are recorded properly, as individual interests or objectives may change during different stages or phases of the program. Goals may need to be adjusted depending on plateaus and other setbacks.

Determine Availability of Facilities and Equipment

Whether to begin a program at home, at school, work, or at a commercial center is a decision facing most potential weight lifters. Often the location of the workout is chosen by default, as there may be limited options available to the individual. However, the accessibility of facilities and equipment is an important factor in deciding where and potentially when to workout.

Home equipment offers the convenience of minimal travel, as well as the luxury of constant availability of equipment. Also, home equipment can be customized based on the needs and financial resources of the lifter. Disadvantages include initial cost of equipment, availability of space, and potential for interruption at home. Often home equipment is utilized extensively after the initial purchase, but sporadically utilized after the novelty of the exercise program has diminished.

School-based facilities generally have the advantage of an extensive amount of equipment, but usually a large number of individuals are competing for exercise space or equipment. Universities generally offer excellent facilities, and the costs are built in to student service fees. High schools provide athletic facilities, or smaller facilities utilized for weight training classes.

Many businesses have embraced the concept of corporate fitness and the need for offering exercise facilities for their employees. Companies have often provided their own fitness areas or contracted for memberships at convenient health clubs. Some businesses even offer release time to exercise, knowing that the benefits of fitness for their employees is well worth the time invested in the workout.

Commercial fitness centers offer the convenience of variety of equipment and extensive hours. Also, the facilities will usually have certified trainers to help you begin and develop your program. Drawbacks include cost and location of facility. Depending on the individual living in a large or small town, travel to and from the facility maybe a limiting factor. Accessibility issues often affect the decision to join a fitness facility, and this factor is especially prevalent in the elderly population.

Potentially, lifters may have access to multiple facilities. This offers the advantage of keeping the program diverse as different facilities generally offer a variety of different types of equipment. Utilizing multiple workout centers can help maintain variety in an individual program and assists with the prevention of plateaus or setbacks.

Assess Knowledge and Experience Level

Many individuals will begin a program without prior experience or guidance. They may have read an article or viewed a television show that touted the benefits of weight training, and therefore they feel they are now ready to begin a weight training program. A healthy recommendation would be to seek the advice of a personal trainer or other knowledgeable individual with the experience and education to help design a safe and effective program. Personal trainers should be certified by a reputable certification agency in order to ensure some level of competence in the area of fitness.

The National Strength and Conditioning Association (NSCA) certifies individuals as Certified Strength and Conditioning Specialists (CSCS). An individual with this particular certification should be qualified to assist with many strength development programs. The American College of Sports Medicine (ACSM), American Council on Exercise (ACE), and the National Academy of Sports Medicine (NASM) are all examples of certification agencies that offer their graduates personal training skills. If you are not sure of how to begin a program, it is important to seek someone out who knows!

Review Time-Management Skills

An exercise program is often easy to begin based on the emotional state of the participant. In other words, many individuals will begin a program because of a television show, an advertisement, or simply from the encouragement of another individual (think New Year's resolutions!). However, improvements in strength and fitness do not take place in a short period of time. Long-term continuation of the program is of paramount importance if changes in strength and/or muscle endurance are desired. Continuation of an exercise program does take a certain time commitment from the individual. Many people indicate that they are "busy" in our society, as time demands may "creep" in and take precedence over an exercise program. One key is to prioritize the program into a daily schedule or routine. Make the commitment to exercise on a specific schedule. However, it is wise to maintain the flexibility to modify some workout times based on other family, job, or social commitments.

Choose the Proper Exercises and Routine

By performing a simple Internet search, you will find a multitude of exercise routines and programs, each of these touting the benefits of that particular program. Bookstores have multiple books on weight training routines, and many of these offer sound advice on program development. Magazine shelves are filled with glossy covers of individuals who advertise the benefits of strength and conditioning. However, as each individual is unique in body type and individual goals, care should be used when selecting an appropriate program. Seeking the advice of a competent personal trainer or other knowledgeable individual in order to continue the program is beneficial at this point as well. If individual focus is on upper-body strength, then the program should emphasize the larger pectoralis and latissimus muscles before the arm exercises. If a lifter wishes to work on core stabilization for athletic performance, then those types of exercises should be implemented in the proper order. Many novice lifters will enter the gym and begin exercising using whatever piece of equipment is available, thereby increasing the probability of injury or little or no results.

Maintain Proper Form

Maintaining proper technique is similar to choosing the correct exercises. Both of these will assist the lifter in two ways—achieving results and preventing injury. A novice lifter will often sacrifice technique for increased resistance, meaning that he/she will perform an exercise with too much weight and sacrifice form in the process. Exercises should be performed with the concept of focusing on the specific muscle groups used in the exercise. In other words, "Function will dictate form." The function of the muscle will dictate the form used to train the muscle. The bicep muscle's function is to flex the humeroulnar (elbow) joint. Based on the overload principle, if you contract the biceps against a resistance, those particular muscles will get stronger. However, utilizing other muscle groups (cheating) could result in injury.

The most important piece of advice a beginning weight trainer can use is to "begin gradually." Many novice trainers will be excited about this new venture and attempt to do too much too soon. This can lead to frustration with the program, and in a worst-case scenario can lead to injury as discussed in the previous section.

Recover Adequately

A basic difference between skeletal and cardiac muscle is the recovery time needed after exercise. Multiple sessions without adequate recovery time will lead to little or no gains in strength. Some individuals believe that there are certain skeletal muscles that can be worked on a daily basis. Because cardiac muscle differs from skeletal muscle, it can be worked on a daily basis and experience increased adaptations. However, all skeletal muscle needs a minimum of 48 hours to recover, but this may vary according to the intensity of the exercise (Jones, Bishop, Richardson & Smith, 2006). Adaptations and strength increases will not occur on a significant basis unless sufficient recovery time is provided. The intensity of effort (sets/repetitions/resistance) will also affect the recovery time necessary to achieve gains in strength. A sound weight lifting principle is to train hard, but also rest hard!

Change Program as Needed

The body will quickly grow accustomed to any stress placed on it. The basic training principle of overload is based on this physiological fact. Variety is a very important principle in an exercise program. Once the human body ceases to adapt to the stresses placed on it, further gains will not be possible. This is known as a "plateau." Plateaus are a part of every conditioning program, but their effect can be minimized by changing up the workout whenever it becomes stale. Periodization is based upon the concept that the body will grow accustomed to the load that it is forced to endure. Varying or altering the program (through changing exercises, modalities, or other variables) can facilitate increases in strength and endurance.

MODALITIES OF WEIGHT TRAINING

Resistance training can be accom-plished with any modality (device or instrument) that will overload a contracting muscle. The individual muscle only responds as it is called upon to produce force, so any substance that can resist the muscle contracting can be utilized for strength development. Free weights, (including dumbbells and barbells) are the most common form of resistance exercise. Selectorized (weight stack) and plate loading machines offer an alternative to regular free weights. There are many different types of exercise machines currently on the market today. However, other forms of resistance exercise include rubber bands, rubber tubing, water, individual body weight, or even stationary objects. Recently increasing in popularity in fitness centers are both Kettlebells and body bars. There are advantages and disadvantages to each type of modality. However, the predominant factor in choosing the type of resistance training should be individual goals and preference.

Image courtesy of the author

Kettlebells

© dslaven, 2013. Used under license from Shutterstock, Inc.

Table 2.1   Comparison of free weights and machines

© Francisco Turnes, 2013. Used under license from Shutterstock, Inc.

Free Weights

Advantages	Disadvantages
Versatility	Less safe – higher risk of injury
Build entire body strength	Difficult to maintain proper form
Increase balance	Takes longer to workout – less efficient
Movements incorporate stabilizer muscles' weakest point	Range of motion repetition dictated by
Cost/availability/space requirements	Need spotter for heavy lifts

© Vereshchagin Dmitry, 2013. Used under license from Shutterstock, Inc.

Machines

Advantages	Disadvantages
Easy to use	Generally limited to one part of body
Save Time	May not allow to work on non-dominant-side weakness
Less intimidating	Fixed path – "one size fits all" – possibly hard to adjust
Safety	
Isolation of muscle groups	
Easier to circuit train	Not portable

A kettlebell is basically a spherical weight with a circular handle fastened above it for the grip. They are manufactured in weights ranging from 1–70 pounds.

Benefits of kettlebell training include all of the benefits of conventional resistance exercise. One of the unique aspects of this form of training is the variety of exercises that can be performed without the limitation of a dumbbell. Since kettlebells are easier to control, this allows the lifter many additional movements to incorporate into his/her program. Also, the lifter does not need a great deal of space or expensive equipment to achieve a good workout. Research has shown that kettlebell training can yield positive results in the area of muscle strength and endurance (Manocchia, Spierer, Lufkin, Minichiello & Castro, 2013).

Kettlebells originated many years ago in Russia to help in training the military and Olympic athletes. They are now increasing in popularity and many clubs offer classes with these resistance exercises alone. Kettlebell certification courses have recently become more popular, indicating that this form of resistance exercise is making a comeback in the industry.

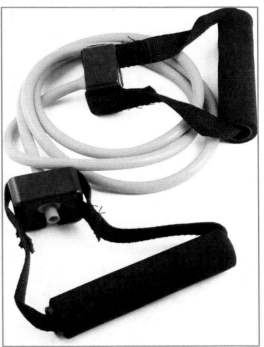

Disadvantages of Kettlebells include the inability of lifters to not prepare their bodies for proper execution of the exercises. The most common area injured in the body while performing these exercises is the lower back.

Bands/Tubing

Resistance bands and tubes have the advantage of being lightweight, inexpensive, portable, and easily adaptable to most muscle groups. A band can be anchored or used in combination with multiple muscle groups. Bands come in various strengths and extensibilities, so it is important to utilize bands that match individual strengths. While bands were originally marketed to a rehabilitation focus, bands have been utilized by all ages and fitness groups to assist with their resistance exercises. Bands will vary the resistance opposite of most free weight exercises, meaning that the further the band is stretched the greater the resistance. Also, bands and tubes allow the exerciser to work in multiple planes of movement, thereby conditioning muscles in a more functional fashion.

Medicine Balls

Medicine balls, similar to Kettlebells, originated many years ago as a fitness modality and have recently also become more popular in gyms. These balls range anywhere from 2–30 pounds and are generally constructed from vinyl or leather. The medicine ball is utilized as a resistance modality primarily by throwing and catching. Advantages

include ease of use (who doesn't know how to throw or catch a ball?) and portability. Medicine balls are basically two types—bouncing and non-bouncing. Any sport that values a quick reaction time would benefit from bouncing medicine ball training. Medicine ball training has been shown to have positive effects on strength in a group of baseball players that combined this training with bat swings (Szymanski, Szymanski, Bradford, Schade & Pascoe, 2007).

Body Weight Exercises

Because resistance exercise can be accomplished by any force that opposes the muscle, body weight exercises are also returning to predominance as an excellent method for increasing strength and endurance. While the standard push-up and chin-up have been utilized for years, exercise programs consisting of body weight exercises alone have recently become more popular. Advantages of body weight exercises include low cost, portability, and ease of use. Disadvantages include limitation of resistance (however, additional resistance can be added to the body), and necessity of additional equipment. Many body weight exercises can be performed with the floor or ground with minimal extra equipment or facilities.

Body Bars

Similar to a weight bar, body bars come in different weights and lengths. This allows the user to perform various activities with a minimum amount of equipment. Popular in group exercise classes, body bars also offer a convenient way to supplement other resistance exercises. These range anywhere from 4–24 pounds, and allow the lifter to perform multiple exercises with an easy-to-grip resistance bar.

Athletes and Sports Performance

Weight training is an important conditioning component for power athletes; however, performance in pure endurance events can be improved with a well-structured strength routine. Besides skill training, nothing can equip an athlete better for enhanced performance than a well-rounded strength and conditioning program. There are obvious differences in the method that each of these athletes would be trained, so it is important that a competent strength and conditioning coach designs a weight training program specific to that athlete's needs.

As athletes have learned the benefits of utilizing resistance exercise, they have also learned new techniques of training to enhance their performance. Weight training with athletes provides several performance related benefits.

© Stefan Schurr, 2013. Used under license from Shutterstock, Inc.

First, the athlete gains size and strength, and in most sports it is a competitive advantage to be bigger and stronger.

Second, weight training can increase power for the athlete. Many sports require power, which is the ability to provide force through a distance in a period of time. An increase in power can help a volleyball player when jumping up to block an opponent's shot, or even a golfer swing a club to create additional club-head speed when striking the ball.

Third, weight training has been shown to increase balance and even enhance coordination with athletes. Balance and coordination are essential elements for almost all sporting competitions.

Fourth, weight training delays muscle fatigue, thereby assisting the athlete in sustaining a high level of performance over a longer period of time. When athletes start experiencing muscle fatigue, proper form is generally compromised and performance deceased.

Finally, weight training helps prevent injury. Stronger muscles mean greater joint strength. Stronger joints are less susceptible to injury. Because weight training can also reduce or delay muscle fatigue (which compromises form), poor form or technique is a contributory cause to many injuries experienced in sports

Weight training: Weight training refers to any activity that involves the use of weights. The term weight training is commonly used to refer to people who lift weights but not for the purpose of competing in bodybuilding, power lifting, or weightlifting (although many people lift weights as a means for improving their performance in another sport).

Resistance training: Resistance training is a broad term because resistance can be supplied by weights, machines, resistance bands, and any number of other devices that resist movement of the exerciser. The main purpose of resistance training is to increase strength, not muscle size.

Weightlifting: Weightlifting has a "generic" meaning that refers to the activity of lifting weights. To those who are well versed in the use of weights, the word weightlifting has a particular meaning. It refers to the Olympic sport of weightlifting, which tests strength and power through two methods of lifting a barbell overhead—the Snatch and the Clean and Jerk. Weightlifting is the only Olympic sport involving weight, and this is why it is sometimes referred to as Olympic lifting or Olympic-style weightlifting.

Bodybuilding: Bodybuilding is a sport or activity in which the primary objective is to develop the size and refine the shape of skeletal muscles. Bodybuilders focus on building muscles proportionally (symmetrically), minimizing body fat and increasing muscle strength. The main objective of bodybuilders is on muscular development, not strength.

Power lifting: Power lifting is a sport conceived as a pure test of strength. The sport consists of three events: the squat, bench press, and dead lift. Power lifters are very strong athletes as they focus on developing that capacity exclusively. Power lifting is not practiced as widely as Olympic-style weight lifting; however, it tests strength about as well as weight lifting.

An individual involved in any of the foregoing activities is considered a weight trainer.

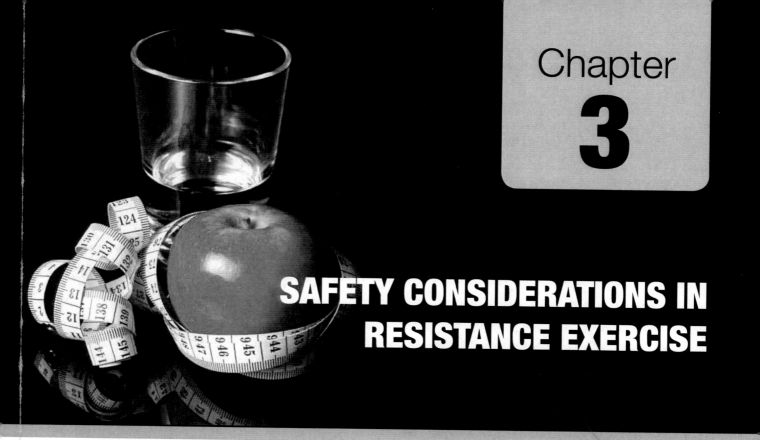

Chapter 3

SAFETY CONSIDERATIONS IN RESISTANCE EXERCISE

MEDICAL CLEARANCE

Before starting any strength training program all individuals should complete a comprehensive physical examination by a qualified physician. A physical examination will help determine if an

© Alexander Raths, 2013. Used under license from Shutterstock, Inc.

individual is healthy enough to engage in a strength training program, and thereby allow a person to have medical clearance to start a program. Medical clearance becomes more important if a person is sedentary, overweight, or older. A physician may be able to identify if an individual has any risk factors that would limit or even prohibit his or her ability to engage in a strength training program.

WHAT TO WEAR

© Yeko Photo Studio, 2013. Used under license from Shutterstock, Inc.

Clothing

Clothing for any individual should be comfortable and allow for freedom of movement while performing the exercises in a full range of motion. Very loose clothing is not recommended because this could pose a danger by getting caught in the equipment. With the various materials available on the market today, a good sweat-wicking material would be recommended to keep an individual cool during his or her exercise program. It is also recommended that a person carry with him/her a towel so that he/she can remove sweat from the equipment he/she comes in contact with in the fitness center. This is common courtesy to all people who use the fitness center, and only takes a few seconds. Some fitness centers even have antibacterial disposable wipes that a person can use after coming in contact with the equipment.

Shoes

Exercise shoes are an important factor when engaging in a strength training program. Proper footwear must be worn at all times while in a fitness center, especially for safety reasons. Examples of shoes would be running shoes, aerobic shoes, or cross-training shoes. An individual should never wear flip-flops or open-toed shoes while lifting weights. A person does not have to buy the most expensive shoes on the market to be able to get the most benefit. It is recommended that a person wear shoes that provide good support throughout the foot (lateral, medial, and arch).

Belts

Strength training belts are used to help stabilize the spine and the lower back to help prevent injury, especially while utilizing free weights. Strength training belts are only recommended for advanced lifters—people lifting very heavy resistance, or individuals

Scenario:

Your training partner indicates you should wear a weight belt because it allows you to lift more weight. How do you respond to this?

with existing back injuries. On certain advanced strength training movements, such as all Olympic lifts and squats, a belt could be used. It should be noted that people should not lift to their maximum ability since there is an increased risk for injury even while wearing a belt. Research studies show that always using a belt for all lifts will not strengthen the core stabilization muscles and could possible weaken the lower back. Strict exercise form and lifting within the ability of the individual will help reduce the chances of lower back injuries; therefore, for the average individual a belt is not recommended while performing basic lifting movements such as machine exercises.

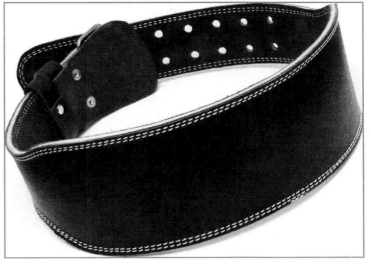

Gloves

Gloves are used by individuals to help protect their hands while lifting weights. Most strength training equipment, especially weight bars, have a rough surface in order to facilitate the lifter's grip on the bar. Not wearing gloves could possibly cause abrasions or blisters on your hands. Gloves should fit tightly and follow the contours of your hand. Select a glove made of a thin material such as leather, or a synthetic blend that allows for full contact between your hand and the equipment. A very thick and padded glove is not recommended because it will not allow for a full grip of the equipment, thereby reducing your sense of touch and may diminish your chances of holding the equipment properly.

Wraps

Wraps are commonly used to help protect and stabilize joints. Most wraps use materials such as athletic tape, elastic bands with Velcro, or neoprene. Some individuals may have an injured joint such as the knee, and a wrap would be recommended. Most Olympic lifters will use wraps to help support and stabilize a joint to prevent injury from heavy lifts; however, for the beginning or basic strength trainer wraps are not necessary.

Lifting Straps

Lifting straps are used to relieve the pressure on the forearm muscles when performing upper- and lower-back exercises. Because the forearm muscles are considerably smaller and not capable of producing much force, the grip tends to be exhausted before the larger primary muscles are fully exercised. By utilizing a pronated or supinated grip on a bar, the extensor and flexor muscles in the forearm serve as prime movers and tend to fatigue first in the exercise. This may limit the larger muscle group's involvement in the exercise.

SAFETY EQUIPMENT

Collars, clips, or springs are various terms used to describe safety equipment that secures weights to a barbell. All of these perform the similar function of making sure the weight does not fall or slide off of the bar. The most widely used term is "collar." A person should always use a collar when lifting with all barbell free weights regardless of the amount lifted. Even if a person is only lifting 10 pounds (a 2 ½-pound weight on each side of a 5-pound bar), collars should always be used. You would want to use a collar on both sides of the barbell to make sure both sides are evenly and properly secured. It is common for a person to become distracted or to lose balance, and the weight could thereby slide off and cause serious injury.

Pads

Pads are used on barbells to help protect the lifter from the hard surface of the bar. Pads are made of durable foam surrounded by a thick, resistant sleeve. The pads have a slit from one end to the next, which makes it easy to install on the bar. Usually the pad is only 12 inches in length and is positioned in the center of the bar. Typically a pad is used for advanced lifters performing a squat with a barbell.

Smith Machine

The Smith Machine was developed by Jack LaLanne and Rudy Smith in the 1950s to assist a lifter on any vertical-type lift. The machine is similar to a squat rack, with vertical guide rods attached to a barbell. The machine allows the barbell to move only straight up and down as it follows the guide rods. The advantage of this type of machine is primarily safety related. The lifter has a built in "spotter" in the machine, allowing him to rack the weights on several prepositioned hooks on the sides of the machine. Also, many of the Smith Machines have counterweights attached to the barbell, thereby offsetting some of the resistance of the barbell.

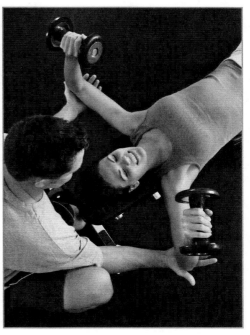

Breathing

An important safety consideration while weight training is proper breathing mechanics. Generally every exhalation should be preceded by a proper inhalation! While this statement may seem obvious, the important consideration should be to remember to breathe normally while lifting. Some lifters have a tendency to hold their breath during either phase of the lift, and this can dramatically increases intra-thoracic pressure in the body. This is known as the Valsalva maneuver. A general recommendation is to "blow the weight up," meaning that an exhalation should occur on the concentric phase of the exercise. An important point is to remember to control the speed of movement of the exercise in order to prevent hyperventilation by breathing in and out too quickly. Lifters should remember to breathe normally during the lift to minimize any potential risks of holding their breath during an exercise.

Spotting

Spotting is a term that refers to the process of closely and intently monitoring an individual while performing a strength training lift. A spotter is a person who is spotting in a direct and close position while monitoring the lift. The main goal of a spotter is to assist the lifter during a failed attempt. The spotter must be in a position so they can immediately assist the lifter if he cannot perform the lift. It is important to use a spotter when working out with free weights, especially with all lifts when weight is being lifted above the head or over the body. Under no circumstance should a person attempt a dangerous lift (above the head or the body) without the use of a knowledgeable and experienced spotter. Not using a spotter could result in serious injury and even death. Typical lifts that always require a spotter are the bench press and the squat. Sometimes it is advantageous to use two spotters during dangerous lifts, where they are positioned on either side of the bar. One of the most important aspects of spotting is effective communication between the spotter and the lifter. Before the lift both the spotter and the lifter should clearly communicate the following:

- What strength training movement to be performed
- How many repetitions the lifter will attempt
- Does the lifter need a lift-off to get the weight into starting position
- A countdown to when the lifter will start the lift
- How much assistance the lifter may need during the lift
- The signs, signals, or words the lifter will use to communicate during the lift.
- At the end of the lift if the lifter needs help guiding the weight back on to the rack

Guidelines and Responsibilities of the Spotter

1. To be strong enough to help in the case of a failed lift. If the spotter is not strong enough a second or different spotter may be required.
2. To understand the proper form of the strength training lift to be performed.
3. To be prepared and focused at all times during the lift. It is crucial that the spotter closely watches the entire lift and should never take his eyes off the lifter.
4. To be ready at a moment's notice to help in the attempt of a failed lift and immediately assist the lifter.
5. To maintain a proper spotting and lifting position during the entire lift.
6. To not touch the bar during the lift if the lifter is able to perform the correct form and is able to lift the weight. By touching the bar during the lift you could unbalance the bar and jeopardize the lifter's safety. Also, by touching the bar a spotter could also possibly either decrease or even increase the overload stimulus of the lifter.
7. To check that the weight is evenly balanced on both sides and that the collars are properly secured.
8. To ensure a clear area around the lifter's feet so he does not to trip or lose balance.

Guidelines of the Lifter

1. Clearly communicate to the spotter so he knows what to expect.
2. Do not assume the spotter knows exactly what you are going

to perform; if he is unaware then it would be the fault of the lifter for not communicating it before the lift.

3. Do not quit or stop at any time during the lift. During a failed lift, continue to attempt the lift 100% to help the spotter get the weight back on the rack.

4. Never completely let go of the bar during a failed lift even if the spotter is touching the bar.

5. Always politely thank the spotter at the end of each lift.

OTHER SAFETY GUIDELINES AND FITNESS CENTER ETIQUETTE

Many people may utilize a fitness center at the same time, making it crowded and hectic. This is why it is important to follow some basic safety guidelines and etiquette while exercising in a fitness center. While most people do not follow basic fitness center safety and etiquette, it is important that you adopt these following guidelines for appropriate behavior in a fitness center to make the experience better for you and the people around you. Who knows—maybe they will take notice and start to follow your example!

1. Always come prepared and wear the correct clothing.

2. Make sure you practice good personal hygiene. Make sure you shower, use deodorant, brush your teeth, and wear clean clothes for sanitary reasons.

3. If you have a fever or are contagiously sick, do not visit a fitness center. It is better to recover at home and not get others sick.

4. Do not engage in lifting exercise of the body part that is inured. It is better to rest and recover than potentially injure the body part more. No pain, no gain is *not* the proper philosophy.

5. Never chew gum or use smokeless tobaccos while exercising in a fitness center.

6. Do not wear strong perfume, cologne, or body sprays while exercising.

7. Keep the volume of your headphones to a reasonable level; if someone needs to get your attention (in the case of a spotter), you will be able to hear him/her.

8. Always carry a towel and wipe down equipment after each use.

9. Bring your own water bottle so you can stay hydrated during your exercise session.

10. Refrain from using profanity, rude comments, or jokes that could be offensive to others.

11. Refrain from loud grunting and yelling while attempting a lift; this can be distracting, upsetting, and alarming to others.

12. Refrain from bringing and using a cell phone (talking and texting) while in a fitness center. This can be distracting to others. Also, this will help reduce the chances of your cell phone being damaged by moving weights.

13. If you do not know how to use a piece of exercise equipment make sure you ask a qualified instructor or employee how to properly use the equipment.

14. Rerack all weights. Fitness center clutter is very annoying and it makes for an unsafe environment. Also, this courtesy makes it much easier for everyone to find the correct weights in the proper place.

15. Before reracking the weight on a bar or piece of equipment, look around first and ask politely if anyone was using that piece of equipment. Someone may still be using that piece of equipment!

16. Do not rest on the equipment between sets. Move off the equipment and ask others if they would like to work in with you between sets.

17. It is appropriate to ask politely if you can work in between sets with another person who is using a piece of equipment that you need to use.

18. If you do work in with another person, then it is polite to notice the weight he was using, and once you are finished with your set to return the weight to the previous setting the person was using.

19. Do not drop weights, hit dumbbells together, or slam the plates on a weight machine together.

20. Ask politely for a spot and be ready to attempt the lift. Do not take extra time to focus on the lift, since you are taking time from another person's workout.

21. Always thank a spotter after performing a lift.

Do not attempt to lift more weight than you can handle.

22. Graciously accept if an individual asks you for a spot and you can safely lift the weight. If you are not able to safely lift the weight, then decline or ask if another person can assist you in the spot.

23. No matter how clean a fitness center may seem, multiple people are touching the same equipment as you. Make sure you keep your hands away from your face and mouth to prevent contracting viruses and bacteria.

24. If a fitness center has disposable antibacterial wipes, then use them after each time you come in contact with a piece of equipment. This will help prevent the spread of germs.

25. At the end of your entire exercise routine make sure you immediately wash your hands with soap and water for 30 seconds.

Scenario:

You roommate wants to go workout with you and he is leaving the dorm room with sandals and cut-off shorts. What advice could you give him and why?

DEVELOPING A STRENGTH TRAINING PROGRAM

TYPES OF MUSCLE CONTRACTIONS

During resistance exercise there are two types of muscle contractions that can occur: isometric, or a static contraction, and isotonic, or a dynamic contraction. The first part of the word "iso" means equal, or same. Metric means length or measurement and tonic

means tone or tension. Therefore an isometric contraction ("same length") is when there is no change in muscle length; hence there is no muscle movement. An isotonic contraction ("same tension") occurs when the muscle changes length, but there is no change in resistance.

In an **isometric or static contraction**, there is no change in muscle length even though the muscle is generating force. For example, force would be generated against an immoveable object such as a wall. A person could push against a wall and the muscle would contract but it would not be able to change length because it would not overcome the resistance. Isometric contractions can produce great strength gains, but they are very ineffective for strength training since they would only be gaining strength at the particular angle the muscle was generating force. However, a good example of incorporating isometric muscle contractions would be on a long-distance flight in an airplane. If a person was on a flight for 15 hours, he/she could perform some simple isometric contractions with his/her legs to keep blood flowing in the leg muscles. The benefit of this would be to reduce deep-vein thrombosis, which can occur when a person sits for long periods of time. Also, exercises such as a "plank" utilize an isometric contraction in order to increase core strength and stabilization.

During an **isotonic or dynamic contraction** the muscle changes length while generating force, while the tension or resistance stays the same. Dynamic muscle contractions are what most people perform when they engage in a strength training program at a fitness center. In most of the exercises machines and all of the free weights, the resistance stays the same while the muscle changes in length. An example of this would be a person grabbing a 10-pound dumbbell and performing a bicep arm curl. The bicep muscle would change length both by shortening and lengthening while the resistance stays the same, resulting in a dynamic exercise.

CONCENTRIC CONTRACTION/ POSITIVE RESISTANCE

A **concentric muscle contraction** occurs when the muscle shortens in length. Using the same example as the bicep arm curl, when the bicep shortens in length it is lifting the dumbbell upwards. This will also result in flexion of a joint. **Flexion** occurs in a joint that when the angle in a joint decreases, or gets smaller. This is also the time when an individual should exhale during the exercise.

ECCENTRIC CONTRACTION/ NEGATIVE RESISTANCE

An **eccentric muscle contraction** occurs when the muscle elongates. Again, in the bicep arm curl, when the bicep elongates the dumbbell is lowered; this is also called "negatives." The purpose of an eccentric contraction is to lower the resistance in a slow, deliberate, and controlled manner. This will result in extension of a joint. **Extension** occurs in a joint when the angle in a joint increases, or gets larger. An individual should inhale during this portion of the exercise.

To review, concentric and eccentric relate to muscle length, while flexion and extension relate to the angle of a joint.

BASIC STRENGTH TRAINING PRINCIPLES

Overload Principle

The **overload principle** is the foundation for all strength training programs. The overload principle occurs when the stress and demands placed on a muscle or muscle group are greater than normal.

Progressive Overload Principle

The progressive overload principle states that when you systematically and progressively increase the stress placed on a muscle over time, this will cause a positive physiological adaptation to occur. Essentially you must force the muscle to work harder than normal to see results. Factors involved in progressive overload are resistance (weight), repetitions, sets, frequency, and rest. If you worked out with a 10-pound dumbbell for the bicep arm curl for an entire year and you did not change resistance, repetitions, sets, frequency or rest, then it is unlikely that any increases in strength will occur.

Repetition

A **repetition** is the movement of one exercise through its full range of motion; for example, performing a full movement of the bicep arm curl with both concentric and eccentric muscle movements.

Set

A **set** is a group of repetitions followed one after another for a given exercise. One set of the bicep arm curl could be 10 repetitions.

Resistance

Resistance is the amount of load, or the weight that is lifted during a given exercise.

Rest

Rest is the time or duration between sets. For example, if an individual were performing 2 sets of 10 repetitions, then they would rest 60 seconds between the two sets. The amount of rest between sets is very important depending on an individual's goals.

Frequency

Frequency is the number of training sessions per week. For example a person might train three times a week. The important point regarding frequency is there should be 24–48 hours rest between strength training sessions; specifically, you need to have at least one day of rest before you exercise the same muscle group.

Specificity of Training

Specificity of training indicates that sport training should be relevant to the activity that the individual wishes to perform Relating this to resistance exercise, this can mean that an individual must exercise specific muscles in order to achieve results for that particular muscle; for example, to improve the biceps muscle group an individual would perform a bicep arm curl exercise. However, specificity may include individual tolerance to the load or stressors, recovery time, and outside commitments as well.

Volume

Volume is the sum of all repetitions, sets, and resistance during an entire strength training session. For example, if an individual performed 3 sets of 15 repetitions of 10 pounds for the bicep arm curl the training volume would be 450 pounds (3 × 15 × 10).

Periodization

Periodization is the designing and structuring of a strength training program into phases. These three phases are macrocycles, mesocycles, and microcycles. This form of training cycles the training based upon the goals of muscular endurance, hypertrophy, and strength.

BUILDING A PROGRAM FOR YOUR SPECIFIC GOALS

Muscular Endurance

Muscular endurance is the ability of a muscle to exert submaximal force repeatedly over time. The goal of muscular endurance training is to build muscles that are lean and toned, thereby facilitating the development of endurance; this is the most common and recommended style of strength training for the beginner. The objective is to perform high repetitions at a low intensity to improve the muscular endurance.

© Mircea BEZERGHEANU, 2013. Used under license from Shutterstock, Inc.

Muscular Hypertrophy

Muscular hypertrophy training increases the size of the muscles on the body. **Hypertrophy** is defined as the increase in the size of muscle fibers. It is to be noted the hypertrophy is not the increase in the *number* of muscle fibers. If a person wants to get "bigger or larger" muscles, then he would focus his training program on hypertrophy training. In a muscular hypertrophy phase, an individual performs medium–high resistance with a medium number of repetitions.

© niderlander, 2013. Used under license from Shutterstock, Inc.

Muscular Strength

Muscular strength is the ability of a muscle to generate maximum force against a heavy resistance in very few repetitions. The ability to lift the heaviest amount of weight or resistance is the goal of a muscular strength program. In a muscular strength phase an individual lifts high resistance with low repetitions. This program is only recommended for advanced strength training individuals due to the high risk by lifting maximum resistance.

For most beginning or recreational strength training individuals, they will be able to achieve muscular en-durance, muscular hypertrophy, and muscular strength. As long as an individual follows the progressive overload principle and periodization, they will be able to make gains in all three areas.

Table 4.1 Muscular Endurance, Growth, and Strength Variables

Training Variable	Endurance	Hypertrophy	Strength
Sets	1–3	4–5	6 or more
Reps	12–15	8–12	Less than 8
Resistance	<70%	71–80%	>80%
Rest between sets	30–60 seconds	60–90 seconds	120 seconds
Frequency per week	2–3 times per week	3–5 times per week	4–6 times per week
Rest between workouts	1–2 Days	1–2 Days	1–2 Days
Duration of Workout	30–60 min	30–60 min	30–60 min

ORDER OF EXERCISES

The order of exercises is very important in the success of a strength training program. There are three fundamental rules to follow for the order of exercises.

- Train large muscles before small
  - Small muscles fatigue before larger muscles. If you exercise your smaller muscles before larger muscles they would fatigue first, making it more difficult to perform exercises using large muscles.
  - For example, chest or back before arms
- Perform multijoint before single joint
  - Performing multijoint exercises
  - For example, squat before leg extension
- Alternate between push and pull exercises
  - For example, chest press followed by seated row

Program Design

Program design for a beginner is crucial in order to achieve results. The reason why most individuals do not achieve results is because they do not have a solid and accurate program design for strength training. Not having a detailed program design will not allow the body to physiologically adapt to the stress placed upon the muscles. Too many times an individual will randomly select exercises, weight, sets, and reps only to be disappointed in not achieving results. An individual must systematically follow a detailed program design in order to achieve results.

Starting Resistance

It is important to select a correct starting resistance or weight for any beginning strength trainer. One of the biggest mistakes an individual can make is to select too heavy of a resistance at the start of his/her program. If an individual selects too heavy of a weight, then he/she risks the chance of injury, or more likely suffering from delayed-onset muscle soreness, or DOMS. **DOMS** is an overuse muscle injury resulting in micro-tears in the muscle fibers, which cause muscle damage. The soreness that an individual feels after a day or two of training is the result of DOMS. If a person follows a strict program design and selects the correct starting weight, then he/she will reduce the chances of encountering DOMS. The best recommendation for a starting weight is to select a weight that you can easily perform. The starting weight an individual selects should almost feel effortless. The reason for selecting a light resistance is to be able to learn to perform each exercise correctly. Also, this allows your body to gradually adapt to this new type of stress placed upon the body. An individual should also progress slowly to keep the risk of injury and the muscle soreness to a minimum.

Week 1 The goal for Week 1 of the program design is to learn the exercises and to determine a starting weight. If an individual does not know what weight to start with, then he/she should always choose the lightest weight; this will reduce the chances of DOMS. The focus for Week 1 is to **Perform 1 set of 15 repetitions** of the lightest weight for each of the exercise; this will allow for the muscles to slowly adapt to the stress placed upon them.

Week 2 The goal for Week 2 is to slowly and gradually increase the sets performed. An individual will add a second set for Week 2, keeping the resistance the same as Week 1. The focus for Week 2 is to **perform 2 sets of 15 repetitions of light weight for each exercise**.

Week 3 The objective for Week 3 is to develop a solid foundation for an individual to build upon. The primary goal for Week 3 is to develop muscular endurance. Muscular endurance is the ability to perform repeated repetitions over an extended period of time and resist fatigue. The program design for Week 3 will increase the sets to 3, increase weight, and decrease reps; hence an individual will **perform 3 sets of 8 repetitions of a moderate weight for each exercise**. After Week 3 the program design will focus on progressive overload along with periodization.

Week 4 Week 4 will maintain 3 sets of the same resistance of each exercise but will increase the repetitions to 10.

Week 5 Week 5 will maintain 3 sets of the same resistance of each exercise but will increase the repetitions to 12.

Week 6 Week 6 will maintain 3 sets of the same resistance of each exercise but will increase the repetitions to 15.

Week 7 After Week 7 the program design starts over, which is incorporating periodization (cycles). For Week 7 an individual will continue with 3 sets, but will increase the weight from Week 6, and reduce the repetitions to 8.

Here is a summary of the progressive overload program design incorporating periodization.

- Week 1   1 set of 15 repetitions of light weight
- Week 2   2 sets of 15 repetitions of light weight (same resistance)
- Week 3   3 sets of 8 repetitions of moderate weight (heavier than that of Week 2)
- Week 4   3 sets of 10 repetitions same weight as Week 3
- Week 5   3 sets of 12 repetitions same weight as Week 4
- Week 6   3 sets of 15 repetitions same weight as Week 5
- Week 7   3 sets of 8 repetitions, slight increase in weight from Week 6. Cycle starts over
- Week 8   3 sets of 10 repetitions same weight as Week 7
- Week 9   3 sets of 12 repetitions same weight as Week 8
- Week 10   3 sets of 15 repetitions same weight as Week 9

Here is a sample of performing the chest press with correct progression over 12 weeks in an exercise log.

		Week 1		Week 2		Week 3	
	Sets	Weight	Reps	Weight	Reps	Weight	Reps
	1	75	15	75	15	100	8
	2			75	15	100	8
	3					100	8
Chest Press		Week 4		Week 5		Week 6	
	Sets	Weight	Reps	Weight	Reps	Weight	Reps
	1	100	10	100	12	100	15
	2	100	10	100	12	100	15
	3	100	10	100	12	100	15

		Week 1		Week 2		Week 3	
	Sets	Weight	Reps	Weight	Reps	Weight	Reps
		Week 7		Week 8		Week 9	
	Sets	Weight	Reps	Weight	Reps	Weight	Reps
	1	110	8	110	10	110	12
	2	110	8	110	10	110	12
	3	110	8	110	10	110	12
Chest Press		Week 10		Week 11		Week 12	
	Sets	Weight	Reps	Weight	Reps	Weight	Reps
	1	110	15	120	8	120	10
	2	110	15	120	8	120	10
	3	110	15	120	8	120	10

TYPES OF STRENGTH TRAINING ROUTINES

Strength training routines are determined by the level and goal of the individual. Beginners will have a different routine than a competitive strength trainer, and a competitive strength trainer will be different than an athlete. The following is a list of sample routines.

Full Body Routine

Most individuals will follow a full body routine, especially people engaging in a beginning strength training program. A **full body routine** focuses on performing all of the major muscle groups of the body in one single exercise session, with a day of rest between exercise sessions. This typically results in a 2–3 day per week exercise frequency. This a very effective and efficient program design for the beginner.

The following is a simple full body strength training program following the correct order of exercises, utilizing both machine exercises and free weights.

1. Machine chest press
2. Seated rowing
3. Overhead shoulder press
4. Lat pull-down
5. Leg press machine
6. Knee extension quadriceps
7. Knee flexion hamstrings or leg curl
8. Seated biceps arm curl dumbbell
9. Lying triceps extension

Split Routine

A more advanced strength training program is the split routine program. A **split routine** allows for an individual to perform exercises based on muscular groups. An example of this would be an upper body and lower body routine. This would result in a 4 day frequency program design. Monday and Thursday an individual would perform upper body only exercises, while on Tuesday and Friday he/she would perform lower body exercises, with a rest day being on Wednesday. There are various other scenarios for a split routine for strength training. Below is another example of a 5 day split routine.

- Monday and Thursday   Chest and triceps exercises
- Tuesday and Friday   Back, biceps, and shoulders exercises
- Wednesday   Leg exercises

Fixed Routine

A **fixed routine** is one in which the variables (sets, reps, and resistance) are not changed during an exercise session. An example of a fixed routine would be performing 3 sets of 10 repetitions of the same weight. The sets, reps, and weight are the same for each exercise. It is to be noted that the weight will change based on the muscle group that is targeted, but the sets and repetitions will be the same.

Circuit Routine

A **circuit routine** is when an individual follows a specific sequence or circuit performing one exercise and then moving to the next exercise until he/she has completed all of his/her exercises. Then the routine could be repeated two or three times. The basis of this program is to reduce the rest time between each exercise. It is recommended to follow a push/pull program by alternating between pushing and pulling strength training exercises. The benefit of this routine allows for maximum utilization of time while at a fitness center.

Pyramid Routine

In a **pyramid routine** the weight for each set is either increased or decreased based upon the repetitions. There are two types of pyramid routines: a regular pyramid routine or an inverted pyramid routine. In a regular pyramid routine an individual would start with high repetitions with light weight, and then increase the weight on each subsequent set while decreasing the repetitions. In an inverted routine an individual would start with heavy weight and low repetitions, and then decrease the weight and increase the repetitions on each following set. Both of these routines are very effective in producing beneficial results, but should be performed by a more advanced strength trainer. Below is an example of a regular pyramid routine and an inverted pyramid routine.

Regular Pyramid Routine		
Set	Reps	Weight
1	15	100
2	12	110
3	10	120

Inverted Pyramid Routine		
Set	Reps	Weight
1	10	120
2	12	110
3	15	100

Super Set Routine

A **super set routine** involves performing two exercises that stress *opposing* muscle groups with little or no rest between sets. The objective of this routine is to focus on opposing muscle groups such as the biceps and the triceps. An example of this would be performing the bicep arm curl followed immediately by performing the lying triceps extension. This is another efficient and effective strength training routine for the more advanced strength trainer.

Compound Set Routine

A **compound set routine** involves performing two different exercises that stress the *same* muscle group with little or no rest between sets. The objective of this routine is to focus on the same muscle group, such as the biceps. For instance, an individual would perform one set of the seated bicep dumbbell arm curl and then immediately perform a standing barbell bicep arm curl. This is a more advanced routine since the stress placed on a single muscle group is compounded because both exercises utilize the same muscles. Again, this routine is designed for the more advanced strength trainer.

Scenario:

You are asked to help develop a conditioning program for an individual who will be hiking in the Grand Canyon in four months. What advice can you offer regarding an appropriate resistance exercise program to help prepare him/her for his adventure?

GETTING STARTED: WARM-UP, FLEXIBILITY, STRETCHING, AND COOLDOWN

There is a distinct difference between warm-up, flexibility, stretching, and cooldown; however most people believe that these terms are synonymous. This chapter will discuss and illustrate the differences among these different concepts and will point out some important characteristics of each one.

WARM-UP

A warm-up session is important before any individual engages in physical activity. The purpose of a warm-up is to gradually increase the blood flow to the muscles, tendons, and ligaments. Increasing the blood flow to the muscles will increase the internal temperatures of the muscles, which will help improve your performance and help reduce your chances of injury. A proper warm-up should gradually increase heart rate and respiration. A warm-up session consists of performing light aerobic exercises such as the treadmill or an elliptical machine for 5–10 minutes. A specific warm-up would entail performing the activities you are preparing to do, but at a decreased intensity level. The more intense your planned exercise session will be, the more time you will need to spend on the warm-up. An important benefit of a warm-up is that it allows you to perform your stretching exercises. You should always stretch after your warm-up. Contrary to belief, most people think you should stretch before you exercise; however, this is not true. Most research shows that it is more beneficial to stretch after your workout, as stretching immediately before performance may actually decrease muscle strength (Power, Behm, Cahill, Carroll & Young, 2004).

FLEXIBILITY

The degree of movement that occurs in a joint is called range of motion (ROM). Flexibility is a measure of ROM in a joint. Many factors affect a joint's range of motion:

- Genetics
- Age
- Recent physical activity
- Muscle temperature
- Joint structure
- Ligaments and tendons
- Muscle bulk and fat bulk
- Previous injury scar tissue

A proper strength training program should increase or maintain flexibility, not decrease it. Many people think that if an individual participates in a strength training program it will decrease his/her flexibility. But, research shows that a properly designed strength training program including warm-up, stretching, and cooldown will improve flexibility.

STRETCHING

Stretching is a type of exercise that is used to increase the flexibility in a joint. There are various methods of stretching techniques, and some are safer and more effective for improving flexibility. The four methods covered in this text are:

1. Static stretching
2. Ballistic stretching
3. Dynamic stretching
4. Proprioceptive neuromuscular facilitation

Static Stretching

Static stretching involves a slow and constant movement, allowing the muscles to be lengthened gradually through a joint's complete range of motion and held in the end position. Static stretching is recommended for all individuals to increase and improve flexibility in a joint. It is recommended that static stretching be performed after a warm-up. Because static stretching is performed slowly, the chances of injury are reduced. Static stretching exercises are easy to learn and cause little pain, which make them the most common and recommended stretching exercises to perform. There are two types of static stretching, active and passive. Active stretching is when the muscles are lengthened or elongated by a contraction of the opposing muscles. This occurs when the actual individual stretching supplies the force of the stretch; for example, the person lifts the leg while laying down, thus having to contract the hamstring muscle while stretching the hamstring muscle group. A passive stretch occurs when a force is applied by an outside source; for example, a passive stretch occurs when a partner or a stretching machine provides the force for the muscles to be stretched.

Ballistic Stretching

Ballistic stretching is a flexibility exercise that occurs when suddenly and rapidly stretching a muscle with a bouncing or swinging movement. Ballistic stretching requires fast and repetitive bouncing or swinging movements to perform the stretch. Ballistic stretching could possibly result in muscle-fiber tears and cause trauma to the muscle being stretched. Individuals with preexisting lower back or hamstring injuries should not perform ballistic stretching. Due to the risk factors of ballistic stretching, it is only recommended for elite athletes and after a long, proper warm-up. Ballistic stretching is not recommended or preferred for people engaging in a strength training program.

Dynamic Stretching

Dynamic stretching involves speed of movement and active muscular effort to simulate a sport-specific movement. Dynamic stretching is different than ballistic stretching; it avoids rapid bouncing or swinging movements. It focuses more on the speed of the movement and is specific to a sport or a motion. Dynamic stretching is often the preferred method of stretching for elite athletes before an athletic competition; therefore, dynamic stretching is not needed nor recommended for individuals performing a strength training program.

Proprioceptive Neuromuscular Facilitation

Proprioceptive Neuromuscular Facilitation (PNF) is based on contracting and relaxing the muscle and requires the assistance of a partner. PNF stretching is the most beneficial and superior of all types of stretching for any person engaging in exercise; however, it is rarely performed since it is very technical; it takes a longer amount of time and requires a partner knowledgeable in PNF stretching.

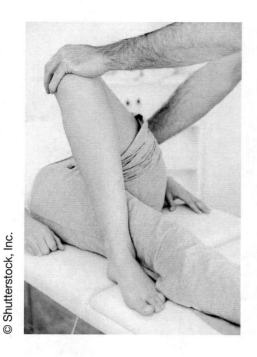

© Shutterstock, Inc.

There are three distinct phases of a PNF stretch:

1. **Passive-Hold Phase.** A partner stretches the muscle group desired to a desired point where the person being stretched can feel the stretch. This position is held for 10 seconds.

2. **Contract Phase.** The individual being stretched then applies a force in the opposite direction of the stretch against the person who is holding the stretch. This will result in an isometric muscle contraction with no movement. It is important to note that no movement should occur during this phase.

3. **Contract-Relax Phase.** After 5 seconds of isometric contraction the person being stretched will relax the muscle being stretched. The partner will then slowly increase the amount of force to the muscle being stretched, thus resulting in a greater ROM of the muscle and joint.

Physiological Adaptations to Stretching

There are two very important sensory organs involved with stretching; these are called proprioceptors. These two proprioceptors are muscle spindles and the Golgi tendon organs. The primary function of these two proprioceptors is to protect the muscle and prevent injury during a sudden muscle stretch.

Muscle spindles are designed to detect a change in muscle length. If the muscle is stretched too fast the muscle spindle is activated and will contract the muscle being stretched. This is known as the stretch-reflex method. After 6 seconds the muscle spindle is deactivated and the Golgi tendon organ is activated.

The Golgi tendon organ performs the opposite response of the muscle spindle, which reduces muscle contraction and increases muscle relaxation. The Golgi tendon organ prevents injury of the muscle being stretched by reducing the tension on the muscle being stretched. This is why it is very important to hold a stretch for longer than 10 seconds in order to deactivate the muscle spindle and to engage the Golgi tendon organ. This illustrates why the PNF technique is so effective in increasing the joint ROM for a muscle.

COOLDOWN

The purpose of a cooldown is to reduce the heart rate back to resting or normal levels after activity. This will assist in recovery and help reduce the chances of fainting or other cardiovascular problems after exercising. A proper cooldown can be accomplished by slowly jogging or walking, followed by stretching.

Therefore, a proper strength and conditioning program should proceed in this recommended order:

1. Warm-up
2. Stretch
3. Exercise
4. Cooldown
5. Stretch

Scenario:

You walk into the weight room and you see your workout partner performing a series of fast, bouncy hamstring stretches before he begins his bench press routine. Can you offer him any advice?

NUTRITION AND WEIGHT TRAINING

A balanced diet is important for our overall health and wellness. Dietary intake is also very important for weight lifters. When to eat and what to eat are factors that will help optimize the benefits of resistance exercise. Although choice and timing are important, minimal effort is needed to maximize the benefits. A fast-paced world, along with poor eating habits, can sometimes make us feel that making the right food choices is next to impossible. A little effort and gradual, minor adjustments can make major differences as we seek to improve our overall health and establish our weight lifting program. Maximizing our choices based on sound knowledge of nutrition can alleviate the fear one may have of having to rely completely on costly supplements, gimmicks, or many of the prepared-meal programs that are gaining in popularity. Therefore, some nutritional knowledge can be of great assistance in the supermarket, and can save us money as we college students try to stretch our dollars. The goal of this chapter is to give you the valuable information you need as a weight lifter to make sure you attain maximal benefits from your training program.

THE NUTRIENTS

There are six categories of nutrients needed by the human body. The macronutrients are the energy (calories) providing nutrients—protein, carbohydrates, and fats.

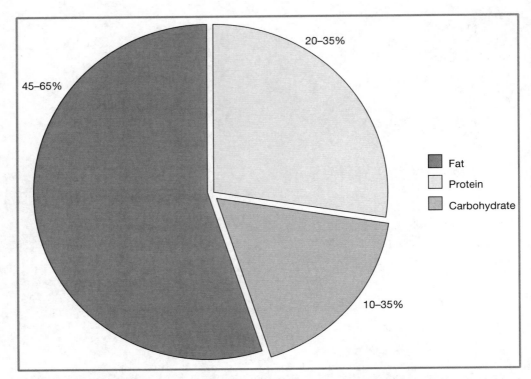

Figure 6.1 Recommended Calories from the Macronutrients (From *Fitness for Living* by Bill Hyman, Gary Oden, David Bacharach, and Tim Sebesta. Copyright © 2011 by Kendall Hunt Publishing Company. Reprinted by permission.)

The micronutrients—vitamins, minerals, and water—do not provide energy (calories). Figure 6.1 illustrates the percentages of the macronutrients recommended for a balanced diet, compared to the percentages in the current American diet.

PROTEINS

Proteins are important and discussed first as they pertain to weight lifters. Proteins are the major building blocks in the human body and are major components of nearly every human cell. They play an important role in the development of antibodies, enzymes, blood, skin, bone, and muscle. Proteins also supply the body with energy in the absence of available carbohydrates and fats. Like carbohydrates, they provide 4 calories per gram. Proteins are made up of amino acids. There are 20 amino acids that the human body uses, 9 of which are called essential because the body cannot manufacture them. The other 11 amino acids are called nonessential because they can be manufactured by the human body. A high-quality protein, or complete protein, is one that contains all 9 essential amino acids and comes from animal sources. Plant-source protein does not contain all of the essential amino acids and is called an incomplete protein. Incomplete proteins, however, can be combined so that all necessary amino acids are provided. Digestibility is also important in regards to protein sources. Milk protein (casein and whey), egg whites, and soy protein are excellent sources of protein based on your body's ability to digest them. Proteins should make up 10–35 percent of total calories. Guidelines for selecting protein sources are found in Figure 6.2.

10 tips
Nutrition
Education Series

with protein foods, variety is key

ChooseMyPlate.gov

10 tips for choosing protein

Protein foods include both animal (meat, poultry, seafood, and eggs) and plant (beans, peas, soy products, nuts, and seeds) sources. We all need protein—but most Americans eat enough, and some eat more than they need. How much is enough? Most people, ages 9 and older, should eat 5 to 7 ounces* of protein foods each day.

1 vary your protein food choices
Eat a variety of foods from the Protein Foods Group each week. Experiment with main dishes made with beans or peas, nuts, soy, and seafood.

2 choose seafood twice a week
Eat seafood in place of meat or poultry twice a week. Select a variety of seafood—include some that are higher in oils and low in mercury, such as salmon, trout, and herring.

3 make meat and poultry lean or low fat
Choose lean or low-fat cuts of meat like round or sirloin and ground beef that is at least 90% lean. Trim or drain fat from meat and remove poultry skin.

4 have an egg
One egg a day, on average, doesn't increase risk for heart disease, so make eggs part of your weekly choices. Only the egg yolk contains cholesterol and saturated fat, so have as many egg whites as you want.

5 eat plant protein foods more often
Try beans and peas (kidney, pinto, black, or white beans; split peas; chickpeas; hummus), soy products (tofu, tempeh, veggie burgers), nuts, and seeds. They are naturally low in saturated fat and high in fiber.

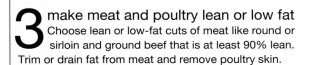

6 nuts and seeds
Choose unsalted nuts or seeds as a snack, on salads, or in main dishes to replace meat or poultry. Nuts and seeds are a concentrated source of calories, so eat small portions to keep calories in check.

7 keep it tasty and healthy
Try grilling, broiling, roasting, or baking—they don't add extra fat. Some lean meats need slow, moist cooking to be tender—try a slow cooker for them. Avoid breading meat or poultry, which adds calories.

8 make a healthy sandwich
Choose turkey, roast beef, canned tuna or salmon, or peanut butter for sandwiches. Many deli meats, such as regular bologna or salami, are high in fat and sodium—make them occasional treats only.

9 think small when it comes to meat portions
Get the flavor you crave but in a smaller portion. Make or order a smaller burger or a "petite" size steak.

10 check the sodium
Check the Nutrition Facts label to limit sodium. Salt is added to many canned foods—including beans and meats. Many processed meats—such as ham, sausage, and hot dogs—are high in sodium. Some fresh chicken, turkey, and pork are brined in a salt solution for flavor and tenderness.

* What counts as an ounce of protein foods? 1 ounce lean meat, poultry, or seafood; 1 egg; ¼ cup cooked beans or peas; ½ ounce nuts or seeds; or 1 tablespoon peanut butter.

USDA United States
Department of Agriculture
Center for Nutrition
Policy and Promotion   **Go to www.ChooseMyPlate.gov for more information.**

DG TipSheet No. 6
June 2011
USDA is an equal opportunity provider and employer.

Figure 6.2   ChooseMyPlate Guidelines for Protein

CARBOHYDRATES

Carbohydrates are the body's preferred form of energy for sustaining daily activity and are very important, along with protein intake, for someone lifting weights. Carbohydrates supply 4 calories per gram, and high-carbohydrate foods typically provide substantial amounts of other important nutrients as well, specifically vitamins and minerals, along with dietary fiber. Most high-carbohydrate foods, which include fruits, vegetables, and whole-grain products, are considered nutrient dense and should make up 45–65 percent of one's daily caloric intake. A nutrient-dense food is one that contains relatively high levels of nutrients packed into a relatively low number of calories. A good example of a specific nutrient-dense food is spinach. One cup of the cooked vegetable provides only 7 calories and virtually no fat, yet is an excellent source of vitamins A, C, E, K, and B-6. It is also an excellent source of riboflavin, potassium, magnesium, folate, and antioxidant carotenoids. On the other hand, a non-nutrient dense food is a typical bag of potato chips, weighing in at 155 calories for 1 ounce (approximately 10 chips) and 10 grams of fat, 3 grams of which are saturated. It is almost completely void of any valuable nutrients.

FATS

Dietary fat has been vilified, but we all need fat in our diet. Approximately 20–35 percent of our calories should come from fat. The problem people encounter is too much saturated fat. Fats provide an avenue for the transportation and storage of fat-soluble vitamins (A, D, E, and K) and are important in the regulation of certain body functions. They help form cell membranes and hormones. They add flavor to food and provide satiety, or that satisfied feeling of fullness that we like to experience after a meal. Many foods containing fat are good sources of high-quality protein needed for weight lifting. Fats also provide energy at a rate of 9 calories per gram, making them the most concentrated form of energy for the body. Yet, while an excellent source of concentrated energy, this also makes fat the fattening nutrient, and anyone interested in losing weight will certainly need to watch his/her fat intake. A good goal for fat intake is between 20–35 percent of total calories. Refer to Table 6.1 for guidelines on fat intake.

WATER

Sometimes considered the forgotten nutrient, water is as important as the other nutrients. Once water enters the body, it mixes with other compounds, primarily minerals, to produce fluids critical to all life processes. These body fluids transport important nutrients and other substances to the cells, carry waste away from cells, and allow

Table 6.1 Cutting the fat

The following substitutions are helpful in reducing dietary fat. The comparative grams of fat are shown for some items.

Instead of:	Try
Butter or margarine	Butter substitutes
Regular yogurt	Non-fat yogurt
Regular salad dressing	Non-fat salad dressing
Mayonnaise	Mustard or low fat salad dressing
Tuna in oil	Tuna in water
Fried foods	Baked or broiled foods
Dark meat poultry	Light meat poultry
Prime beef	Choice or select beef
Bacon and sausage	Lean ham
Burger and fries	soup and salad
Pepperoni pizza	Canadian bacon pizza
Whole milk dairy products	Skim or low fat dairy products
Regular cheese	Low fat cheese, skim milk mozzarella
Pastries (38 g or more)	Hot cereals (2 g)
Muffins (5–12 g)	English muffins (1–2 g)
Croissant (12 g)	Bread (1 g)
Fried chicken (30 g)	Grilled chicken (3 g)
Fried potatoes (12 g)	Baked potato (trace)
In cooking:	**Try**
1 cup of oil	1 cup of applesauce
Whole eggs (6 g)	Two egg whites (trace)
When reaching for a snack:	**Try**
Candy bar	Fresh fruit
Ice cream bars (8–30 g)	Frozen fruit bars (0 fat)

(Continued)

Table 6.1 Cutting the fat (*Continued*)

The following substitutions are helpful in reducing dietary fat. The comparative grams of fat are shown for some items.

Ice cream (11–18 g)	Sherbet, low-fat yogurt, or ice milk (2–4 g)
Doughnuts (14 g)	Bagels (2 g)
Devil's food cake	Angel food cake
High fat cookies and crackers	Fat-free cookies and crackers
Fried corn and potato chips	Baked chips or pretzels

From *Fitness for Living* by Bill Hyman, Gary Oden, David Bacharach, and Tim Sebesta. Copyright © 2011 by Kendall Hunt Publishing Company. Reprinted by permission.

chemical reactions to take place in the body. They lubricate joints, absorb shock, and provide smooth movement during lifts. Water also serves as a solvent for minerals, vitamins, amino acids, glucose, and other substances, regulates body temperature, and maintains blood volume. As you can see, sufficient water consumption for adequate hydration is very important to good health. The average person consumes and excretes (through the kidneys, lungs, and skin) about 2.5 liters of water each day. To assure proper balance, and to avoid dehydration when excessive water is lost, it is important to replace this water loss. Many foods, specifically fruits and vegetables, have high water content and can help replace water loss. While information on the necessary amount of water consumption varies greatly, it is recommended that about 6 to 8 glasses (8 ounces a glass) of water be consumed each day.

© Shutterstock, Inc.

Table 6.2	Facts about vitamins			
Vitamin	**Major Functions**	**Signs of Prolonged Deficiency**	**Toxic Effects of Megadoses**	**Important Dietary Sources**
Fat-Soluble				
Vitamin A	Maintenance of eyes, vision, skin, linings of the nose, mouth, digestive and urinary tracts, immune function	Night blindness; dry, scaling skin; increased susceptibility to infection; loss of appetite; anemia; kidney stones	Headache, vomiting and diarrhea, dryness of mucous membranes, vertigo, double vision, bone abnormalities, liver damage, miscarriage and birth defects, convulsions, coma, respiratory failure	Liver, milk, butter, cheese, and fortified margarine; carrots, spinach, cantaloupe, and other orange and deep-green vegetables and fruits contain carotenes that the body converts to vitamin a
Vitamin D	Aid in calcium and phosphorus metabolism, promotion of calcium absorption, development and maintenance of bones and teeth	Rickets (bone deformities) in children; bone softening, loss, and fractures in adults	Calcium deposits in kidneys and blood vessels, causing irreversible kidney and cardiovascular damage	Fortified milk and margarine, fish liver oils, butter, egg yolks (sunlight on skin also produces vitamin D)
Vitamin E	Protection and maintenance of cellular membranes	Red blood cell breakage and anemia, weakness, neurological problems, muscle cramps	Relatively nontoxic, but may cause excess bleeding or formation of blood clots	Vegetable oils, whole grains, nuts and seeds, green leafy vegetables, asparagus, peaches; smaller amounts widespread in other foods

(Continued)

Table 6.2   Facts about vitamins (*Continued*)

Vitamin	Major Functions	Signs of Prolonged Deficiency	Toxic Effects of Megadoses	Important Dietary Sources
Fat-Soluble				
Vitamin K	Production of factors essential for blood clotting	Hemorrhaging	None observed	Green leafy vegetables; smaller amounts widespread in other foods
Water-Soluble				
Vitamin C	Maintenance and repair of connective tissue, bones, teeth, and cartilage; promotion of healing; aid in iron absorption	Scurvy (weakening of collagenous structures resulting in widespread capillary hemorrhaging), anemia, reduced resistance to infection, bleeding gums, weakness, loosened teeth, rough skin, joint pain, poor wound healing, hair loss, poor iron absorption	Urinary stones in some people, acid stomach from ingesting supplements in pill form, nausea, diarrhea, headache, fatigue	Peppers, broccoli, spinach, brussels sprouts, citrus fruits, strawberries, tomatoes, potatoes, cabbage, other fruits and vegetables
Water-soluble Thiamin	Conversion of carbohydrates into usable forms of energy, maintenance of appetite and nervous system function	Beriberi (symptoms include edema or muscle wasting, mental confusion, anorexia, enlarged heart, abnormal heart rhythm, muscle degeneration and weakness, nerve changes)	None reported	Yeast, whole-grain and enriched breads and cereals, organ meats, liver, pork, lean meats, poultry, eggs, fish, beans, nuts, legumes

Vitamin	Major Functions	Signs of Prolonged Deficiency	Toxic Effects of Megadoses	Important Dietary Sources
Water-Soluble				
Riboflavin	Energy metabolism; maintenance of skin, mucous membranes, and nervous system structures	Cracks at corners of mouth, sore throat, skin rash, hypersensitivity to light, purple tongue	None reported	Dairy products, whole-grain and enriched breads and cereals, lean meats, poultry, green vegetables, liver
Niacin	Conversion of carbohydrates, fats, and protein into usable forms of energy; essential for growth, synthesis of hormones	Pellagra (symptoms include weakness, diarrhea, dermatitis, inflammation of mucous membranes, mental illness)	Flushing of the skin, nausea, vomiting, diarrhea, changes in metabolism of glycogen and fatty acids	Eggs, chicken, turkey, fish, milk, whole grains, nuts, enriched breads and cereals, lean meats, legumes*
Vitamin B-6	Enzyme reactions involving amino acids and the metabolism of carbohydrates, lipids, and nucleic acids	Anemia, convulsions, cracks at corners of mouth, dermatitis, nausea, confusion	Neurological abnormalities and damage	Eggs, poultry, whole grains, nuts, legumes, liver, kidney, pork
Folate	Amino acid metabolism, synthesis of RNA and DNA, new cell synthesis	Anemia, gastrointestinal disturbances, decreased resistance to infection, depression	Diarrhea, reduction of zinc absorption, possible kidney enlargement and damage	Green leafy vegetables, yeast, oranges, whole grains, legumes, liver
Vitamin B-12	Synthesis of red and white blood cells; other metabolic reactions	Anemia, fatigue, nervous system damage, sore tongue	None reported	Eggs, milk, meat, liver

(Continued)

Table 6.2 Facts about vitamins (*Continued*)

Vitamin	Major Functions	Signs of Prolonged Deficiency	Toxic Effects of Megadoses	Important Dietary Sources
Water-Soluble				
Biotin	Metabolism of fats, carbohydrates, and proteins	Rash, nausea, vomiting, weight loss, depression, fatigue, hair loss; not known under natural circumstances	None reported	Cereals, yeast, nuts, cheese, egg yolks, soy flour, liver; widespread foods
Pantothenic acid	Metabolism of fats, carbohydrates, and proteins	Fatigue, numbness and tingling of hands and feet, gastrointestinal disturbances; not known under natural circumstances	Diarrhea, water retention	Peanuts, whole grains, legumes, fish, eggs, liver, kidney; smaller amounts found in milk, vegetables, and fruits

*Niacin can be made in the body from tryptophan, so this list includes foods containing niacin and/or tryptophan.

From *Dietary Reference Intakes for Energy, Carbohydrate, Fiber, Fat, Fatty Acids, Cholesterol, Protein, and Amino Acids (Macronutrients)*. © 2005 by the National Academy of Sciences. Reprinted with permission from the National Academies Press, Copyright 2005, National Academy of Sciences.

NUTRITION FOR THE WEIGHT LIFTER

Many people mistakenly believe that supplements, along with proper diet, are necessary if they lift weights. Sports supplements have become a multibillion dollar industry based on this misconception perpetuated by false advertising from uninformed individuals and media sources. In fact, individuals who lift weights for strength gains can meet all of their body's needs by consuming a healthy diet. As energy expenditure increases due to lifting weights, energy needs also increase, so the athletic individual commonly consumes a greater number of calories for fuel compared with the less-active person. The percentage of nutrients in the total diet, however, should remain the same, with carbohydrates comprising about 45–65 percent of total calories. Fat should still be kept to about 20–35 percent of the total calories, with protein remaining at 10–35 percent of calories. The key for strength training is when you consume your nutrients. Many individuals in training are concerned that they are not getting enough protein from their diets. However, while protein requirements are higher for athletes, they are not high enough to automatically require protein supplements, since the increase in total caloric consumption more than compensates for any additional needs. The recommended daily protein intake is .8 grams per kilogram of body weight. This recommendation includes a margin of safety high enough to cover almost all individuals. Athletes, however, need 1.2–1.7 grams of protein per kilogram of body weight per day (American College of Sports Medicine, 2007). Even these levels are easily met through the increase in caloric consumption needed to meet a highly active person's energy needs (Neiman, 2011). Eating more protein will not build muscle faster—in fact, it may contribute to body fat. On page 59, Laboratory 6.1 is provided to help you determine your daily protein needs.

NUTRITIONAL SUPPLEMENTS FOR WEIGHT LIFTERS

According to the American Dietetic Association (2011), about 40 percent of Americans take vitamin supplements. There is always the question of whether or not supplements are needed for weight lifters. The goal is to obtain proper nutrition from the food sources themselves and not rely heavily or at all on supplements. Supplements are costly, and many individuals taking supplements do not need them in the quantity they are ingesting them. The two supplements that can assist weight lifters if they are not obtaining the proper nutrition from food are whey protein and creatine. Whey protein is absorbed very quickly and is important post-workout. It is also inexpensive in powder form and can easily be mixed with an easily digestible carbohydrate. Whey protein is not needed if you eat egg whites or other lean meats post-workout. Creatine monohydrate is one of the most popular supplements used by weight lifters. Creatine monohydrate turns into creatine phosphate in the body. Creatine phosphate is needed to make adenosine triphosphate (ATP), which provides energy for muscle contractions. Creatine is an amino acid needed for energy production. Your liver, kidney, and pancreas are

© Shutterstock, Inc.

responsible for producing approximately half of your creatine; the rest can be obtained from animal sources (1 pound of beef contains 5 grams of creatine). Fish is also an excellent source of creatine. Many weight lifters mix 3–5 grams of creatine post-workout with whey protein and a simple carbohydrate to accelerate absorption.

While there are varied opinions concerning the necessity of supplements, most nutrition scientists agree that needed vitamins and minerals are easily attainable through a balanced diet. Some individuals believe that if some nutrients are good, then more must be better, but there is no evidence that this is the case. In fact, individuals who insist on supplementing their nutrient intake should exercise caution, since there is a possibility of too high an intake of certain nutrients, especially the fat-soluble vitamins A, D, E, and K. While the water-soluble vitamins B and C are not stored in fat and any excesses are readily excreted, fat-soluble vitamins are stored in the fatty tissue of the body. Continued high intake of fat-soluble vitamins can lead to a dangerous accumulation of these substances, causing a condition known as vitamin toxicity. Kidney and liver damage, as well as other health problems, can result from the consumption of these megadoses of vitamins and some minerals. High levels of some nutrients may also interfere with the absorption of other crucial nutrients; therefore, any supplement that supplies greater than 100 percent of the DRI for any vitamin or mineral is discouraged.

The "pill mentality" is another risk of supplementation. This refers to the mind set that efforts to consume a good diet are unnecessary because nutritional needs can be met by popping a pill. Clearly, a pill is no substitute for a balanced diet, and consuming a supplement does not correct the problems found in a high-fat, high-calorie diet.

Recommendations for Weight Lifters

- Select an eating pattern that meets specific nutrient needs over time at an appropriate calorie level.
- Consume sufficient proteins before and after (fat-free milk, whey protein with a minimum of 3 grams of the amino acid leucine) workout to maximize strength gains. Your body really needs amino acids along with easily-digestible carbohydrates right after your workout.
- Consume fast-acting carbohydrates post workout along with whey protein to maximize protein synthesis.
- Spread your protein intake over 5–6 meals a day to not overload your system with protein in one meal.

YOUR PLAN OF ACTION

Now that you are more aware of the necessary steps for good nutrition to maximize your weight training program, you can incorporate these steps into your personal plan of action.

1. **Eat a balanced meal before and after you workout!** – Sufficient protein mixed with a readily digested carbohydrate will maximize your workout. Eggs are recommended instead of meat because the egg is easily and quickly digested when your body needs the nutrients. It is also important to eat a protein-rich meal right after you workout when your muscles need it most.

2. **Set some specific goals** – Identify foods that will maximize your weight training program. Do not try to make drastic changes in a short period of time because this is very difficult to maintain over time. Then set goals to consume more, or less, of those food items that you identified for change. By maintaining awareness of these two changes, you are more likely to make wiser choices.

3. **Read food labels** – Along with reviewing fat intake, review closely the amount of protein in each food item and make sure it is a good source to maximize your strength training program. Therefore, you can identify nutrient-dense foods through label reading and attempt to consume those foods more often.

4. **Do not overeat or super-size when eating out.** – Portion sizes continue to increase, and it is important to keep this in mind when ordering, regardless of the minimal increase in cost. The few extra pennies to super-size it can wreak havoc on your caloric intake. Also, do not feel you have to overeat if you go to a buffet. Think about making smart food choices with the selections available instead of feeling you have to have more food to maximize the cost you paid for the buffet.

Table 6.3   Good sources of protein for weight lifters
Eggs (preferably egg whites to reduce fat and cholesterol from egg yolk)
Lean, non processed, beef, pork, poultry or seafood
Low-fat dairy products (low-fat or skim milk)
Lentils (kidney beans, chick peas, etc.)
Nuts (walnuts, peanuts, almonds, cashews)
Yogurt and cottage cheese

chapter 6
LABORATORY 6.1

Protein Worksheet:
Calculating Your Daily Protein Needs

The Recommended Dietary Allowance for protein is .8 grams of protein per kilogram of body weight per day. You can calculate your specific protein needs by using the worksheet:

1. Convert your body weight in pounds to kilograms. Since there are 2.2 pounds in a kilogram, the equation is:

   Body weight in pounds ÷ 2.2 = body weight in kilograms

   If John weighs 175 pounds, his weight in kilograms would be:
   175 ÷ 2.2 = 79.5 (or 80) kilograms

   Body weight in pounds _____ ÷ 2.2 = _____ body weight in kilograms

2. Multiply your weight in kilograms by .8. John's protein needs would be:
   80 × .8 = 64 grams of protein per day.

   Body weight in kilograms _____ × .8 = _____ grams of protein needed each day

   Sixty-four grams of protein supply 256 calories. If John is consuming approximately 12 percent (10–15 percent is the recommendation) of his calories from protein, he is consuming plenty of protein in only 2100 calories per day.

3. If John is a highly active individual who believes he requires more than the recommended .8 grams per kilogram per day, he may choose to base his protein needs on 1.2 grams per kilogram per day:

   80 – 1.2 = 96 grams of protein per day.

   Body weight in kilograms _____ × 1.2 = _____ grams of protein possibly needed for a strength or endurance athlete in heavy training

   These 96 grams of protein now provide 388 calories. If protein now comprises about 12 percent of his total calories, this would result in a daily caloric consumption of about 3200 calories per day. If he is indeed a strength or endurance athlete in heavy training, his additional energy expenditure will require at least this many calories.

From *Fitness for Living* by Bill Hyman, Gary Oden, David Bacharach, and Tim Sebesta. Copyright © 2011 by Kendall Hunt Publishing Company. Reprinted by permission.

MUSCLE AND MUSCLE FIBERS

STRUCTURE OF SKELETAL MUSCLE

Skeletal muscle fibers can be categorized two principal ways. The differences occur in the type of the contractile protein myosin (fast or slow), and the degree of oxidative phosphorylation that the fiber undergoes. Muscle fibers can be broken down into two broad categories, generally referred to as Type I and Type II. Type I fibers appear red due to the presence of the oxygen-binding protein myoglobin. Type I fibers are suited for endurance and are slow to fatigue. These fibers use oxidative (aerobic) metabolism to generate ATP. Type II fibers are white due to the absence of myoglobin and a reliance on glycolytic (anaerobic) enzymes. Type II fibers can be divided into subtypes; IIa and IIb (sometimes referred to as IIx). Type II fibers use both oxidative metabolism and anaerobic metabolism depending on the subtype of the fiber. Type IIa fibers have both oxidative and glycolytic capabilities. These fibers are used for prolonged anaerobic activities that require a relatively high force output, such as running a 400-meter race. Type IIb fibers are quickly fatigued and are used for short anaerobic, very high-intensity activities such as sprinting or a one-rep max while lifting weight.

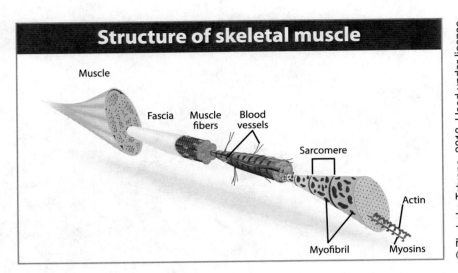

Structure of skeletal muscle

Muscle

Fascia Muscle fibers Blood vessels

Sarcomere

Actin

Myofibril Myosins

© Zhabska Tetyana, 2013. Used under license from Shutterstock, Inc.

Most skeletal muscles in the body are a mixture of all three types of muscle fibers, but their proportion varies depending on the usual action of muscle. Muscles that are constantly active and require a small amount of tension are mostly Type I, while muscles that need to produce a large amount of tension are Type IIa and IIb. For example, postural muscles have a higher proportion of Type I fibers, while muscles that are not constantly active, such as the muscles in arms and shoulders, have a higher proportion of Type IIa and IIb fibers (insert Ref).

Even though all skeletal muscle is a mixture of all three fiber types, all the fiber type of any one motor unit (a motor unit is a nerve and the muscle fibers that the nerve stimulates to contact) contacts

Table 7.1 Characteristics of the three muscle fiber types

Fiber Type	Slow Twitch (ST)	Fast Twitch A (FT-A)	Fast Twitch B (FT-B)
Contraction time	Slow	Fast	Very fast
Size of motor neuron	Small	Large	Very large
Resistance to fatigue	High	Intermediate	Low
Activity used for	Aerobic	Long term anaerobic	Short term anaerobic
Force production	Low	High	Very high
Mitochondrial density	High	High	Low
Capillary density	High	Intermediate	Low
Oxidative capacity	High	High	Low

all the same fiber type. In addition, different muscle fibers are used in various ways depending on need. If only a weak contraction is needed, such as lifting a spoon, thenType I fibers will be used. If a stronger contraction is needed, such as lifting a chair, then Type IIa fibers will be used. During a maximal contraction, such as lifting a piano, Type IIb fibers will be recruited.

Research studies have reported some interesting facts concerning the percentages of slow- and fast-twitch muscle fibers found in humans. There appears to be no difference in the basic fiber distribution of men and women. Also, age does not seem to affect fiber distribution as well. The average individual possesses approximately 50 percent slow-twitch and 50 percent fast-twitch fibers. Successful athletes typically possess a large percentage of one type of fiber. Sprint or power athletes possess a large percentage of fast-twitch fibers, whereas endurance athletes generally have a high percentage of slow-twitch fibers (insert Ref).

If a person desires to know his/her muscle-fiber type, then the procedure is performed by an invasive muscle-biopsy test. During the test a needle is stuck into the muscle and few fibers are plucked out to be examined under a microscope. An indirect method that can be used in the weight room to determine fiber composition of a muscle group is to initially establish a person's 1 repetition max. Perform as many repetitions as possible at 80 percent of his/her one repetition maximum, (1RM). If he/she does fewer than 7 repetitions, then the muscle group should consist of mostly fast-twitch fibers. If between 7 and 12 repetitions are performed, then the muscle group has an equal proportion of fast twitch and slow twitch. If more than 12 repetitions are performed, then the muscle group consists of primarily slow-twitch fibers (Insert Ref).

Fiber type will play a significant role in the amount of weight that a person can lift and the number of repetitions a person can complete in a set. In addition, fiber type plays a major role in the desired outcome of a training program. A person with mostly slow-twitch muscle fiber will never be able to attain as high a level of strength gains as a person with mostly fast-twitch fibers. Likewise,

Table 7.2 Typical muscle fiber composition in Elite Athletes		
Sport	% slow Fibers (Type I)	% Fast Fibers (Type IIx and IIa)
Distance runners	70–80	20–30
Track sprinters	25–30	70–75
Nonathletes	47–53	47–53

Data from references 20 and 82.

Your sister has had a successful track career as a sprinter, and has achieved some very fast times in the 100-meter dash. Now that she is out of high school, she wants to complete a marathon. Do you think she will be as successful in the marathon as she was in her sprints?

a person with mostly fast-twitch fibers will never be able to attain as high a level of muscular endurance as will the person with mostly slow-twitch fibers. It is important to know that regardless of fiber-type composition, a person can improve in both strength and endurance with the proper workout program. Please refer to Chapter 4 for the proper intensity needed for improvement in muscle strength and endurance.

Muscle fiber types cannot be changed. Training for either strength or endurance can change some of the characteristics of the fibers; however, the type of fiber you are born with will largely be maintained throughout your life.

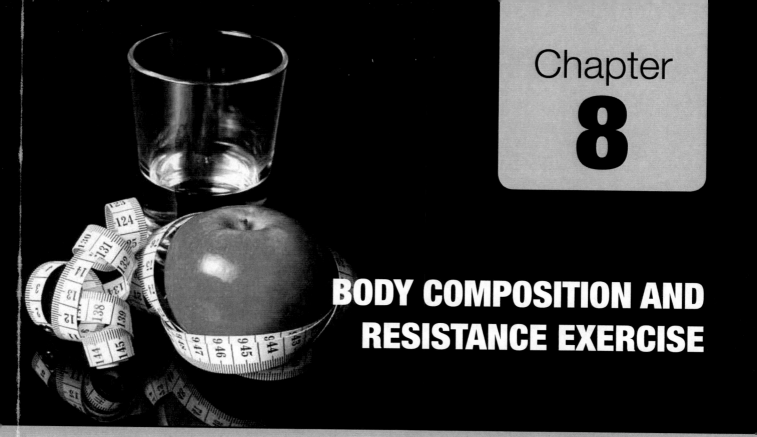

Chapter 8

BODY COMPOSITION AND RESISTANCE EXERCISE

An important consideration in the development of overall fitness is body composition. Body composition refers to the percentage of an individual's lean tissue (muscle) and adipose tissue (fat). While

© iofoto, 2013. Used under license from Shutterstock, Inc.

Table 8.1	Body fat levels by gender	
Classification	Males	Female
Essential fat	3%	12%
Ideal fat	15%	22%
Overfat	16–24%	23–31%
Obese	>25%	>32%

Obesity is generally defined as 10% body fat above ideal.

strength training has been shown to be an effective mechanism for increasing muscle mass, most exercise programs rely on aerobic exercise to decrease fat; however, there is increasing evidence that a properly administered resistance exercise program can also contribute to the reduction of body fat.

It is necessary for humans to have a certain amount of fat in order to exist and regulate specific body functions. This fat is known as essential fat. Essential fat generally makes up approximately 3 percent of individual mass on males and can range from 10–14 percent of the mass in females. Ideal body fat is the percentage of fat that most individuals should strive to achieve. This level of body fat is conducive to good health and the general regulation of body functions. The term "overfat" is used to describe an individual with a percentage of body fat that puts the individual at greater risk for developing disease and potential decreased functional abilities. This is not to be confused with the term "overweight," as these may have two entirely different meanings. Overweight means too much <u>mass</u> for individual height. Overfat means too much <u>fat</u> for individual height; therefore, a bodybuilder may be "overweight" but not necessarily overfat. If someone's body fat levels exceed overfat levels, then they may be considered obese. Obesity is generally defined using Body Mass Index (BMI) values. BMI is mathematically expressed as individual weight in kilograms divided by individual height in meters squared; however, because BMI only measures a height-to-weight ratio, it is not an accurate assessment of body fat because it does not account for the composition of the mass of the individual.

SOMATOTYPE

An individual's basic body type can have an influence on his/her fat distribution. The basic build of an individual's body is referred to as "somatotype" (Sheldon & Stevens, 1942). There are three general

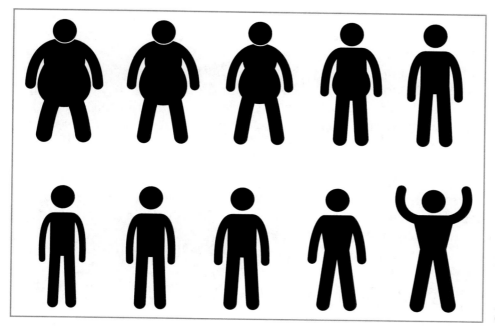

© Leremy, 2013. Used under license from Shutterstock, Inc.

somatotypes, based on the general body build and genetic makeup of the individual.

Ectomorph – An ectomorph is an individual with a lean, slightly muscular body build. This individual will be generally considered "skinny" and more suited to endurance type of activities

Mesomorph – A mesomorph's body type is increased muscle mass and a minimum of body fat. The mesodermal tissues of the embryo predominate this type of build. These individuals would excel in athletic events requiring increased musculature.

Endomorph – An endomorph is an individual with a body build that is predominantly a round, soft type of build. This body type results from the embryonic endodermal tissues. Athletically these individuals are the type of build that a sport such as sumo wrestling would embrace.

MUSCLE MASS AND ENERGY EXPENDITURE

Total energy expenditure (TEE) is a product of an individual's basal metabolic rate (BMR), the thermic effect of digestion (TE), and the quantity and quality of physical activity (PA). Muscle has a dual effect in burning calories in an individual. Skeletal muscle is a metabolically active tissue, utilizing approximately 35 calories per pound per day; therefore, an increase in the amount of muscle mass will have a positive effect on daily calories burned. Also, the greater amount of muscle, the greater increase in the quantity and quality of physical activity available to the individual. One of the benefits of a well-rounded conditioning program is the future ability to sustain activity, both short and long term. This process becomes especially important as we age, due to the inevitable loss of skeletal muscle through sarcopenia.

In an older and aging population, the maintenance of muscle mass is extremely important for the maintenance of health. Aging is associated with the loss of fat-free mass and an increase in body fat (Tzankoff & Norris, 1977). An excessive amount of fat has been associated with several metabolic diseases, including diabetes, hypertension, and hypercholesterolemia (Carnethon, Gidding, Nehgme, Sidney, Jacobs & Liu, 2003); however, research has shown that a strength training program can increase lean body mass and also decrease regional and total fat mass in middle-aged and older men (Treuth, Ryan, et al., 1994).

The quality of the resistance exercise may have a determination on body composition. In a sedentary population, individuals who begin an exercise program generally achieve greater results at the onset of the program; however, in a group that has been training for quite some time, further gains and benefits are more difficult to achieve. A circuit weight training program can assist in changing body composition while at the same time increasing muscular strength (Gettman, Ayres, Pollock & Jackson, 1978). Also, a high-intensity training protocol appears to have a positive effect on body composition, possibly due to the increased aerobic activity that takes place during the exercise session (Westcott, 1996). Because the human body grows accustomed to any stress placed on it, changing the program is often recommended to avoid staleness or plateaus; therefore, high intensity training may offer an alternative

© holbox, 2013. Used under license from Shutterstock, Inc.

Circuit weight training picture

to the lifter as a different method of training. However, the number of sets does not appear to affect the overall body composition of the lifter (Galvao & Taaffe, 2005). These studies reinforce the fact that the quality of the program may be more important than the quantity, or volume of the program.

DETERMINING INDIVIDUAL BODY FAT LEVELS

It is important for several reasons for individuals to know and understand their body fat percentage. First, body fat percentage is an important predictor of health status. Also, this knowledge will assist an individual with goal assessment and measurement toward progress. Body composition can be measured using several different methods. Indirect methods of testing range from a low-cost skin-fold caliper test to the use of an extremely expensive bone density scan called Dual Energy X-ray Absorptiometry (DEXA). Other methods include bioimpedence, underwater weighing, and air displacement. There are advantages and disadvantages to each method of determining body fat percentage.

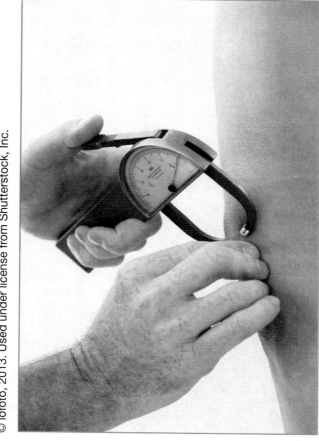

© iofoto, 2013. Used under license from Shutterstock, Inc.

Table 8.2 Body fat measurement methods

Testing Method	Advantages	Disadvantages
Skin-fold calipers	Low cost Easy to perform	Based on accuracy of technician
Bioimpedence	Low Cost Easy to perform	Not accurate in low-fat or high-fat individuals Dependent on hydration status
Hydrostatic weighing	"Gold standard" accuracy	Special facility needed
Air displacement (BOD POD)	Accuracy, time	Cost
Dual energy X-ray absorptiometry (DEXA)	Very accurate	High cost

Scenario:

You are asked to perform body fat measurements at school on your entire class of 85 students. Which method would you use and why?

In conclusion, while a certain level of body fat in necessary to maintain health, most individuals can benefit from reducing their body fat level. A proper strength and conditioning program has been shown to have a direct effect on reducing these levels. Combining strength training with cardiovascular exercise and proper nutritional intake is unquestionably the most effective way to achieve exceptional fitness levels.

DESCRIPTION OF EXERCISES

The exercises illustrated in this chapter represent a basic listing of resistance movements that can be performed in order to increase muscular strength and/or muscular endurance. This is not meant to be a complete list of exercises that can be performed, but this section can offer proper instructions and tips on form to individuals who desire to begin or continue a basic resistance exercise program.

With all of the exercises (especially the dumbbell and barbell lifts) the utilization of appropriate safety procedures is strongly recommended. Please refer to Chapter 3 for guidelines on safety procedures.

While the description of each exercise is meant to be fully instructional, individual differences in machines and weights may necessitate different seat settings, weight adjustments and form adaptations. Please seek the aid of a qualified individual to assist you in the proper utilization of exercise machines at your facility.

Photo courtesy of the author.

LOWER BODY EXERCISES

Leg Press (Basic)

**Major Muscles Involved

1. Quadriceps group
2. Gluteus maximus (buttocks)
3. Hamstrings group

**Execution

1. Place feet on resistance platform (sled) approximately shoulder-width apart, toes at bend in sled pointing straight ahead.
2. Hips and shoulders are pressed against the back support.
3. Buttocks always remains in the seat.
4. Release the holding lever and straighten legs. Do not lock out the knees at any time.
5. Keep the back firmly against the back support. Grasp side handles with hands.
6. Inhale, bending legs to lower the sled at a slow to moderate speed.
7. Lower the sled until the shins are parallel to the floor.
8. Upon reaching the bottom position, press the weight back to the starting position and exhale.
9. Knees are always in line with the toes.
10. Feet are always flat on the platform.
11. Remember to inhale and exhale for every repetition.

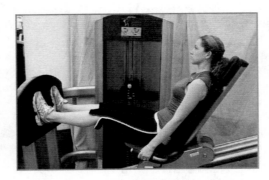

Hack Squat (Basic)

**Major Muscles Involved

1. Quadriceps group

**Execution

1. Place feet on resistance platform approximately shoulder-width apart, toes at the top edge of the platform pointing straight ahead.
2. Back and head are pressed against the back support.
3. Release the holding lever and straighten legs. Do not lock out the knees at any time.
4. Inhale, bending legs, lower the sled at a slow to moderate speed.
5. Lower the sled until the angle of the knees is at 90 degrees.
6. Upon reaching the bottom position, press the weight back to the starting position and exhale.
7. Knees are always in line with the toes.
8. Feet are always flat on the platform.

Squat (Basic)

**Major Muscles Involved

1. Quadriceps
2. Buttocks
3. Lower back
4. Hamstrings (secondary)
5. Middle and upper back (secondary)
6. Abdominal (secondary)

**Execution

1. Use a barbell situated in a squat rack.
2. Place bar across the trapezius and shoulders.
3. Use a wide handgrip on the bar.
4. Lift bar from the rack and take one to two steps backward.
5. Place feet shoulder-width apart, toes angled out slightly.
6. Eyes are focused at eye level throughout the movement.
7. Chest stays up, shoulders held back, back kept straight throughout movement.

8. Slowly bend knees and drop hips back.
9. Descend to a position with thighs parallel to floor.
10. Knees stay over ankles; they never move past the toes.
11. Feet are flat on floor.
12. Slowly press upward to starting position. Do not lock out knees at top of movement.

Jumping Squat (Basic)

**Major Muscles Involved

1. Calves
2. Quadriceps, hamstrings, gluteals

**Execution

1. Use a barbell across shoulders, or dumbbells held at sides.
2. Squat to a parallel thigh position.
3. Spring upward, extending legs all the way through the toes.
4. Enough upward force should be generated to come off the floor.
5. Bend knees to absorb landing back on floor.

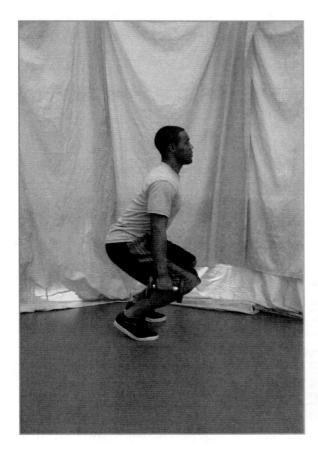
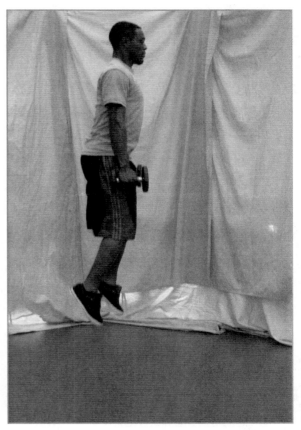

Leg Extension (Isolation)

**Major Muscles Involved

1. Quadriceps

**Execution

1. Adjust back of chair so that bend of the knee is firmly into the edge of the seat.
2. Range of motion should be set at 100%.
3. Roller pad should be set at tops of shoes.
4. Keep the back firmly against the back support and buttocks firmly on seat.
5. Grasp side handles of machine.
6. Inhale, straightening legs to a fully locked position.
7. Exhale, lowering weight to starting position. Do not let lifted weight stack rest against stationary weight stack or slam off stationary weight stack.

Training tip: Focus on final 10–20 degrees of extension

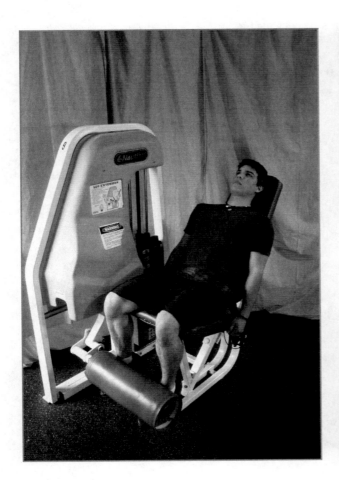 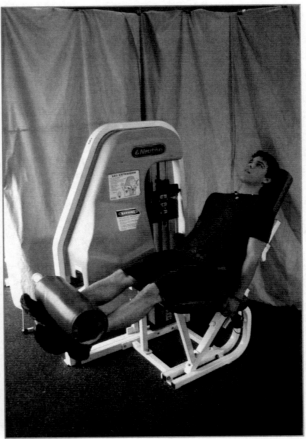

Lying Leg Curl (Isolation)

**Major Muscles Involved

1. Hamstring group

**Execution

1. Adjust roller pads so they will be resting on the ankle just above the shoe.
2. Lie face down on the machine; hook ankles under the rollers. The patella (kneecap) is off the end of the pad.
3. Grasp side handles of machine.
4. Head stays in line with body (do not twist head right or left).
5. Chest stays on pad.
6. Hips stay on pad.
7. Feet stay flexed throughout movement.
8. Curl rollers up with use of hamstrings until rollers touch the buttocks or back of legs.
9. Slowly lower weight to starting position. Do not rest lifted weight stack on stationary weight stack between repetitions.

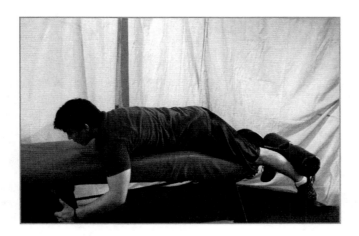

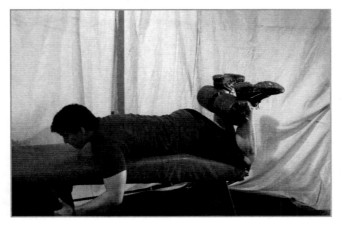

Seated Leg Curl (Isolation)

**Major Muscles Involved

1. Hamstring

**Execution

1. Adjust the ankle pad to be in a position on the back of the ankle just above the shoe.
2. Adjust the back pad so the back of the knee will be firmly against the front of the seat and the knee across from the pivot point of the machine.
3. Sit up tall; do <u>not</u> slouch.
4. Adjust the thigh pad firmly against the top of the thighs.
5. Slowly press down with on the ankle pad using the hamstring muscle group.
6. Return to start position.

The seated leg curl is a good variation to use in place of the lying (prone) leg curl.

Training tip: Avoid locking knees at full extension.

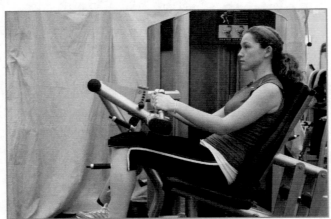

Lunge (Straight Rear Leg) (Isolation)

**Major Muscles Involved

Front Leg

1. Quadriceps
2. Gluteus maximus (buttocks)

Rear Leg (kept straight)

1. Gluteus maximus (buttocks)
2. Hamstrings

**Execution

1. Use a barbell across the shoulders, or dumbbells held in each hand at sides of body.
2. Feet together, eyes looking straight ahead, chest kept up, take a long stride forward with the left foot.
3. Bend the left knee so that the thigh becomes parallel to the floor.
4. If the stride is long enough, the knee should be directly over the foot. The knee should never go past the toes.
5. The right leg is straight throughout the movement.
6. Push hard off the left foot and return to starting position.
7. Alternate legs; each step counts one repetition.

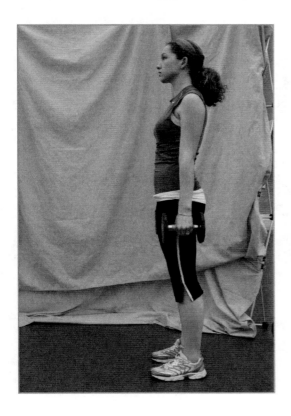

Standing Calf Raise (Isolation)

**Major Muscles Involved

1. Calves (gastrocnemius)

**Execution

1. Face calf machine; place shoulders beneath yokes; stand on platform with toes and balls of feet. Feet should be shoulder-width, toes pointing straight ahead.
2. Lower heels to stretch the calves.
3. Keeping knees locked, rise up on toes as high as possible. Hold this position for two counts.
4. Slowly lower to starting position.
5. Vary the width of the feet and angle of the feet to affect a different training effect on the gastrocnemius.

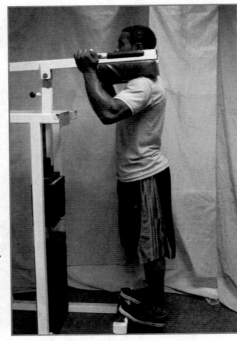 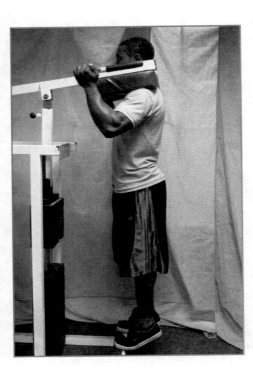

Photos courtesy of John Clark.

Seated Calf Raise (Isolation)

**Major Muscles Involved

1. Calves (soleus)

**Execution

1. Sit down on the machine seat; place toes and balls of feet on platform. If the knee pad does not fit firmly over the top of the knee, adjust.
2. Press up on toes and release retaining bar.
3. Lower heels to stretch the calves and return to a position as high as possible upon toes.
4. Vary width of feet.

UPPER BODY (TRUNK) EXERCISES

Lat Pulldown (Basic)

**Major Muscles Involved
    Front Pull

1. Middle back (middle latissimus dorsi)

**Execution

1. Use a long bar handle.
2. With an overhand grip, place the index fingers outside the rings on the bar, or wider.
3. Knees are placed under the restraint pad.
4. Arms are fully extended at the start and completion of each movement.
5. Arch the lower back; keep the chest up; keep elbows pulling back; slowly pull bar to upper portion of chest.
6. Slowly return bar to starting position.
7. Lean back far enough for bar to clear face.
8. Do not use excess body sway to pull bar down.

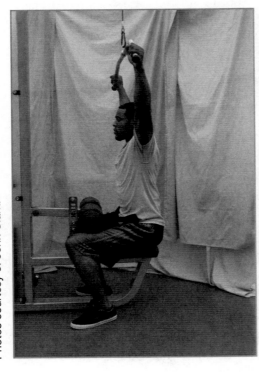 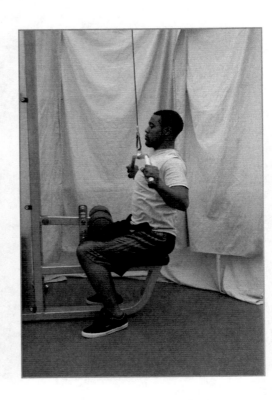

Photos courtesy of John Clark.

Seated Pulley Row (Basic)

**Major Muscles Involved

1. Middle back (lower and middle latissimus dorsi)
2. Biceps

**Execution

1. Use small V-shaped handle.
2. Grasp handle, place feet against foot stops, and sit down.
3. Knees should be slightly bent throughout the movement.
4. To start, straighten arms, lean upper body towards pulley.
5. Simultaneously sit erect and pull handle toward the upper abdomen; keep the lower back arched and chest up.
6. Keep elbows close to sides; pull them as far back as possible.
7. Slowly reverse the procedure and return to starting point.

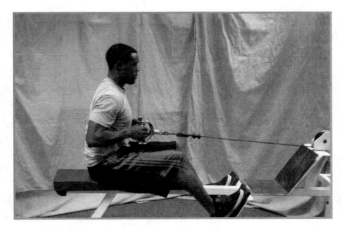

Photos courtesy of John Clark.

Seated Row (Basic)

**Major Muscles Involved

1. Middle back (lower and middle latissimus dorsi)

**Execution

1. Adjust the seat height to a position where the handles, when pulled back, will be at waist height or above.
2. Adjust the chest pad to a position where the weight stack being lifted will <u>not</u> contact the stationary weight stack when the arms are fully extended.
3. Use either the vertical or horizontal handles.
4. An overhand or underhand grip can be used on the vertical handles.
5. Keep the chest up and firmly placed against the chest pad, arch the lower back.
6. Pull the elbows back as far as possible during the lift.
7. Return to the straight arm starting position.

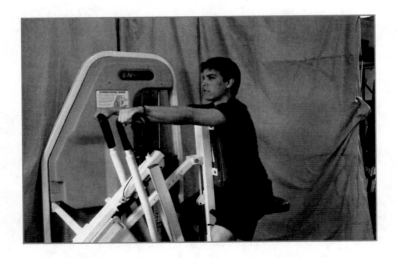

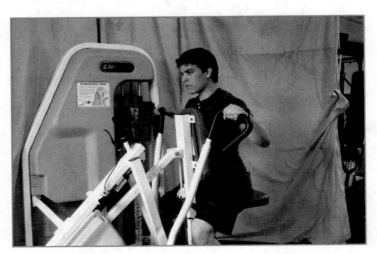

One Arm Dumbbell Row (Isolation)

**Major Muscles Involved

1. Middle back (latissimus dorsi, trapezius, and deltoids)

**Execution

1. Place a DB on the floor next to a bench.
2. Grasp the DB with the left hand.
3. Place right hand and right knee on the bench, left leg kept close to the side of the bench.
4. Torso stays parallel to the floor throughout the exercise. Shoulders stay perpendicular to the floor.
5. Slowly pull the DB upward, keeping the elbow close to the body, until the DB touches the side of the body.
6. Reverse direction to starting position.
7. DB should be slightly forward of the shoulder in the bottom position.

Photos courtesy of John Clark.

Close Grip/Wide Grip Upright Row (Basic—Upper Back, Shoulders)

**Major Muscles Involved

1. Upper back—trapezius (narrow grip)
2. Shoulders—deltoids (wide grip)

**Execution

1. Use curl bar, barbell, or dumbbells.
2. Feet should be shoulder-width, knees kept slightly bent.
3. Grasp bar with an overhand narrow grip (index fingers 4–6 inches apart) to work the upper back, or a wide grip (index fingers just inside shoulder-width) to work the shoulders.
4. Stand erect, arms extended downward, bar resting against upper thighs.
5. Keep the bar close to the body as it is pulled up to a position under the chin.
6. Elbows stay above the level of the hands at all times.
7. Return bar to starting position.

Pull-Up (Basic)

**Major Muscles Involved

1. Middle back (lower and middle latissimus dorsi)
2. Shoulders (posterior deltoid)
3. Biceps

**Execution

1. Take an overhand grip (palms facing out) on the pull-up bar, hands wider than shoulder-width.
2. Straighten arms completely to start and at the bottom of each rep.
3. Arch the lower back, keep the chest up, and pull up until the chin is over the bar or the upper chest touches the bar.
4. Slowly pull up, using the middle back and arms.
5. Slowly return to starting position.
6. Do not swing or use body sway to gain momentum.

Photos courtesy of John Clark.

Shrug (Isolation)

Major Muscles Involved

1. Upper back—trapezius

Execution

1. Use a curl bar, barbell, or dumbbells.
2. Feet should be shoulder-width, knees kept slightly bent.
3. Grasp bar with an overhand wide grip.
4. Stand erect, arms extended downward, bar resting against upper thighs.
5. Shoulders should be forward and down at beginning of each pull.
6. Use upper back (trapezius) strength to shrug the weight upward as high as possible.
7. Arms remain straight throughout movement, bar kept close to body.
8. Do <u>not</u> "roll" shoulders.
9. Return to starting position.

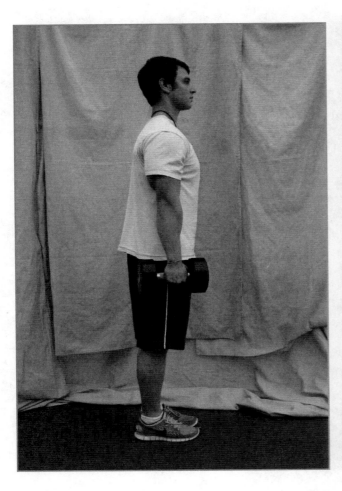 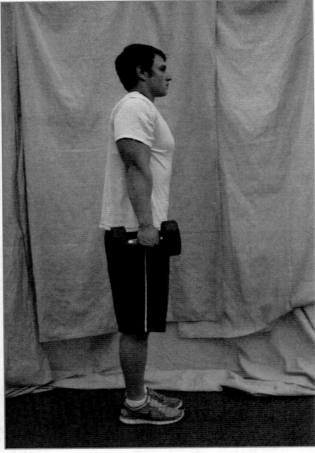

Bench Press (Basic)

**Major Muscles Involved

1. Chest (pectorals, anterior deltoids, triceps)

**Execution

1. Lie flat on the back, feet flat on floor on each side of the bench.
2. Eyes should be 3–5 inches in front of the bar.
3. Use an overhand grip on the bar. Index fingers should be as wide apart as the outer width of the shoulders. The correct hand placement is accomplished when the forearms are parallel to each other as the bar is lowered to the chest. Thumbs are wrapped around bar.
4. Straighten the arms and lift the barbell clear of the rack.
5. Slowly lower the barbell to the chest.
   a. Elbows should be kept wide.
   b. Forearms should be parallel to each other.
   c. Bar should touch nipples.
6. Press bar up and back to starting position.
   a. Feet stay on floor.
   b. Hips stay on bench.
   c. Head stays straight.
   d. Press evenly with both arms.
   e. Press up and back towards rack.
7. Always use a spotter.
8. In order to work the pectorals, it is vitally important to keep the elbows wide, away from the sides of the body, throughout the movement.

 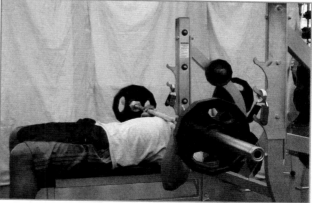

Photos courtesy of John Clark.

Chest Press (Basic)

**Major Muscles Involved:

1. Pectoralis major

**Execution:

1. Lie flat on back with hands gently resting on bar above or in front of you (depending on machine).
2. Extend your arms in a slow, controlled motion.
3. Pause at full extension.
4. Slowly return to start position.

Training tip: Avoid locking elbows.

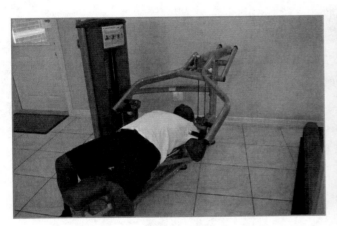 

Incline Bench Press (Basic)

**Major Muscles Involved

1. Upper pectorals, anterior deltoids, triceps

**Execution

1. Same as flat bench press with the following exceptions:
   a. Bar should touch top of pectorals.
   b. The amount of weight used is normally lower than that used for the flat bench press.

Photos courtesy of John Clark.

Decline Bench Press (Basic)

**Major Muscles Involved

1. Lower pectorals, anterior-medial deltoids, and triceps
2. Upper back muscles

**Execution

1. Same as flat bench press with the following exceptions:
   a. Lower bar to touch the lower portion of the pectorals.
   b. The amount of weight used should be greater than that used for the flat bench press.

Photos courtesy of the author.

Close-Grip Bench Press (Basic)

**Major Muscles Involved

1. Triceps (lateral head)
2. Inner pectorals
3. Anterior deltoids

**Execution

1. Use flat bench, barbell, and narrow grip (index fingers 6–12" apart).
2. Feet should be flat on floor or on bench.
3. Eyes should be behind bar with bar on rack.
4. Remove bar from rack using an overhand grip, bar at arm's length above chest.
5. Slowly lower bar to lower portion of pectorals.
6. Slowly press bar to starting position.
7. Elbows stay close to sides of body throughout the movement.
8. An underhand grip may also be used, as it stresses the long and medial head of the triceps.

Fly (Isolation)

**Major Muscles Involved

1. Pectorals

**Execution

1. Flat, incline, and decline flies all have the same execution.
2. Grasp two DB and sit on the end of a bench.
3. Feet flat on floor, lie down on bench, bringing DB to a straight-arm position above the chest.
4. Bend the elbows slightly throughout the movement.
5. The palms of the hands should face each other at the start of the movement.
6. Slowly lower the DB outward and downward in a large semicircular arc.
7. Get a good stretch on the pectorals at bottom of the movement.
8. Slowly reverse direction to starting point.

Shoulder Press

**Major Muscles Involved

1. Deltoid, triceps

**Execution

1. Grasp both handles.
2. Extend your arms in a slow, controlled motion while keeping your back firmly against the pad.
3. Pause at full extension.
4. Slowly return to the start position.

Photos courtesy of John Clark.

Overhead Press (Basic)

**Major Muscles Involved

1. Shoulders (anterior and medial deltoids)
2. Triceps

**Execution

1. Grasp a barbell, overhand grip, index fingers shoulder-width apart, thumbs wrapped around bar.
2. Sit in the overhead press machine or on a flat bench.
3. Hold bar in front of chest at base of neck.
4. Press bar straight overhead to arm's length. Keep bar close to face.
5. Lower bar to starting position.
6. Elbows should be kept directly under the bar throughout the movement.
7. Always use a spotter.

Lateral Raise (Isolation)

**Major Muscles Involved

1. Shoulders (anterior, medial, and posterior deltoid muscles)

**Execution
*Front Laterals

1. Grasp two DBs, standing, feet shoulder-width apart, knees slightly bent.
2. DBs will be resting against upper thighs at start.
3. Have a slight bend in the elbows throughout the movement.
4. Keep upper body as motionless as possible.
5. Raise both DBs forward and upward in a semicircular arc to shoulder level.
6. Lower weight to starting point.

*Side Laterals

1. Same description applies to both side laterals and front laterals.
2. DBs are raised sideward and upward in a semicircular arc to shoulder level.

*Rear Laterals

1. Sit on the end of a bench, feet flat on floor and together, approximately 12–18" in front of bench.
2. Bend forward and place chest on thighs. Chest stays on thighs throughout movement.
3. DBs will be behind feet to start and finish movement.

4. Raise DBs upward and sideward in a semicircular arc.
5. At top of movement the DBs should be across from side of head at arm's length.
6. Lower to starting position.

Rear Deltoid/Pectoral Fly

Rear Deltoid

**Major Muscles Involved

1. Deltoid

**Execution

1. Grasp the upper handles.
2. With your arms extended, elbows slightly bent, pull arms out and back in a slow, controlled motion.
3. Pause at full contraction.

Photos courtesy of the author.

4. Slowly return to start position.

Training Tips: If upper arm travels closer than perpendicular to trunk, latissimus dorsi becomes involved; elbows should be kept same height as shoulders.

Pectoral Fly

**Major Muscles Involved

1. Pectoralis

**Execution

1. Grasp the lower handles.
2. With your arms extended, elbows slightly bent, pull arms forward in a slow controlled motion until your hands meet.
3. Pause at full contraction.
4. Slowly return to start position.

Training Tips: Avoid locking your elbows; set start position so you get full range of motion.

UPPER BODY (ARM) EXERCISES
Standing Barbell Arm Curl (Basic)

**Major Muscles Involved

1. Biceps

**Execution

1. Grasp a curl bar with an underhand grip. Different grip widths can be used.
2. Stand feet shoulder-width, knees slightly bent, and resting curl bar across upper thighs.
3. Keep the upper body from swaying during the movement.
4. Press the upper arms against sides of the body throughout the movement.

5. Curl the bar upward in a semicircular arc to a position under the chin.

6. Keep the wrists straight throughout the movement.

7. Slowly lower bar to starting position.

Alternate Dumbbell Arm Curl (Isolation)

**Major Muscles Involved

1. Biceps

**Execution

1. In a standing position, the feet should be shoulder width apart, back straight, and head level.

2. Grasp dumbbells using an underhand grip, palms facing each other, arms fully extended at your sides.

3. Keep your elbows at your sides throughout the lift.

4. Raise one dumbbell up to the shoulder while rotating the arm so that the palm faces upward.

5. Lower the dumbbell to the starting position and then raise the other arm with the same motion.

Preacher Arm Curl (Isolation)

**Major Muscles Involved

1. Lower section of biceps

**Execution

1. Grasp a curl bar with an underhand grip; vary width of hands.

2. Sit or stand over a preacher bench with upper arms resting upon the surface of the pad.

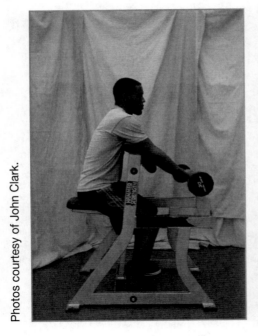
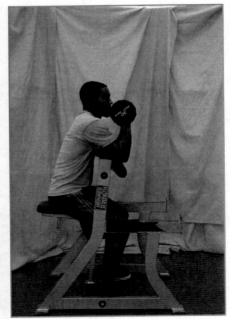

3. The pad should rest firmly in the armpits.
4. Keep a slight bend in the elbow at bottom of movement.
5. Curl the bar upward in a semicircular arc to a position below the chin.
6. Slowly lower bar to starting position.

Concentration Arm Curl (Isolation)

**Major Muscles Involved

1. Biceps (adds height to the outer portion of the biceps)

**Execution

1. Sit on the end of an exercise bench with the feet wider than shoulder width.
2. Using a light dumbbell in the left hand, rest the left triceps against the inner thigh just behind the knee. The right hand can be rested on the right knee.
3. The left arm should be completely straight at the beginning of the movement. Curl the dumbbell to the shoulder, <u>not</u> the chest, twist the hand so the little finger is higher than the thumb, and intensely squeeze the biceps.
4. Return to the start position. Perform the required number of repetitions on the left arm and repeat on the right arm.

Tricep Pushdown (Isolation)

**Major Muscles Involved

1. Triceps (long and medial heads)

**Execution

1. Use a short bar, angled down at the ends.
2. Use an overhand grip.
3. Feet should be shoulder-width, knees slightly bent.
4. Press upper arms into sides of torso throughout the movement.
5. Slowly straighten the arms, moving only the forearms.
6. Squeeze the triceps at the bottom of the movement.
7. Slowly return bar to starting position; elbows never leave sides of torso.

Photos courtesy of John Clark.

Lying Tricep Extension (Isolation)

**Major Muscles Involved

1. Triceps (long and medial heads)

**Execution

1. Use a short straight bar or curl bar.
2. Grasp bar with an overhand grip, index fingers 4–8" apart.
3. Lie back on a flat bench with feet on floor or resting on top of bench.
4. Extend arms directly upward, bar over face.
5. Keep upper arms motionless throughout the movement.
6. Slowly bend arms, allowing the bar to travel downward in a semicircular arc to top of the forehead.
7. Slowly return the bar to starting position.
8. The elbows must stay close together and must not be allowed to travel outward.

 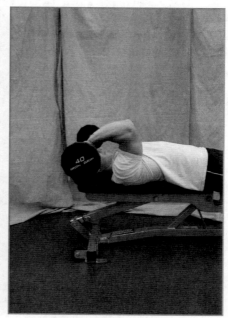

Kickback (Isolation)

**Major Muscles Involved

   1. Triceps (long and medial heads)

**Execution

   1. Use a light dumbbell in your left hand. Place the right hand and right lower leg on a bench. Bend over so the torso is parallel to the floor.

   2. Press the left upper arm against the side of the torso and maintain this arm position throughout the exercise. The upper arm stays parallel to the floor.

   3. The dumbbell should be hanging straight down, elbow at a 90-degree angle.

   4. The palm of the left hand is facing the body.

   5. Slowly straighten the left arm to a point where it is parallel to the floor.

   6. Flex the triceps intensely at the top of the movement.

   7. Return to the starting position.

   8. Perform the required number repetitions on the left arm; repeat on the right arm. This completes one set.

Tricep Extension

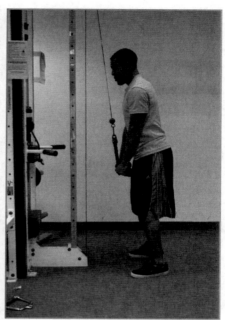

Photos courtesy of John Clark.

**Major Muscles Involved

1. Triceps

**Execution

1. Grasp both handles.
2. Extend your arms in a slow, controlled motion.
3. Pause at full extension.
4. Slowly return to start position.

Training tips: Keep your upper arms flat on the pad; exercise through a full range of motion; adjust seat height so back of upper arms resting on padding.

Overhand-Grip Arm Curl (Basic)

**Major Muscles Involved

1. Forearms

**Execution

1. Use a straight bar or curl bar with an overhand grip.
2. Stand erect, feet shoulder-width, knees slightly bent.
3. The bar will be resting at arm's length across the upper thighs.

4. Keep the upper body from swaying during the movement.

5. Press the upper arms against sides of the body throughout the movement.

6. Keep the wrists straight at all times.

7. Curl the bar upward in a semicircular arc to a position under the chin.

8. Slowly lower the bar to starting position.

Wrist Curl (Isolation)

**Major Muscles Involved

1. Forearm flexor muscles (palms facing up)

2. Forearm extensor muscles (palms facing down)

**Execution

1. Use a barbell or dumbbells.

2. Palms up or down, support forearms on thighs while sitting on bench or, if kneeling by bench, support forearms across bench.

Photos courtesy of John Clark.

3. Hands and wrists are held off the end of the thighs or bench.
4. Let hands drop down as far as possible.
5. Use forearm muscles to curl bar upward as high as possible.
6. Forearms never raise off thighs or bench.

CORE EXERCISES

Leg Raise (Basic)

**Major Muscles Involved

1. Abdominal (rectus abdominis, lower portion)
2. Hip flexors

**Execution

1. Use a chinning bar with an overhand grip, hands shoulder-width. Body should hang straight downward.
2. Utilize abdominal strength to raise legs upward. With knees bent, bring knees as high as possible to the front.
3. Lower legs to a straight position and repeat.
4. Slow, controlled movements will minimize swinging.
5. This exercise can also be performed on a leg raise machine. The forearms support body weight. Knees should be raised above the level of the handles.

 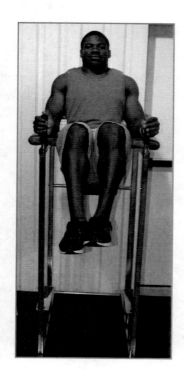

Photos courtesy of John Clark.

Crunch (Isolation)

**Major Muscles Involved

1. Abdominal (entire rectus abdominis)

**Execution

1. Lie with back on floor, legs across a bench, thighs perpendicular to floor, hands behind neck or on chest.
2. Keep the head in the same plane as the back. Do <u>not</u> pull the chin down to the chest.
3. Contract the abdominal muscles and simultaneously lift the shoulders and upper back off the floor.
4. Hold this position for a slow count and lower to starting position.

Photo courtesy of the author.

Rotary Torso

**Major Muscles Involved

1. External obliques

**Execution

1. Select an appropriate weight.
2. Sit with your back against the pad.
3. Adjust range of motion setting to one side.
4. Sit with legs against padding.
5. Rotate torso using waist to opposite side in slow, controlled motion.
6. Pause at full contraction.

Training tips: Use a lighter weight and higher repetitions for the exercise; maintain a loose grasp on the handles during exercise.

Abdominal Curl

**Major Muscles Involved

1. Rectus abdominus

**Execution

1. Sit in machine with back against back support.
2. Place lower legs under pads or on platform.
3. Grab handles above and position hips stationary.
4. Flex waist, bringing elbows forward and down in a slow, controlled manner.

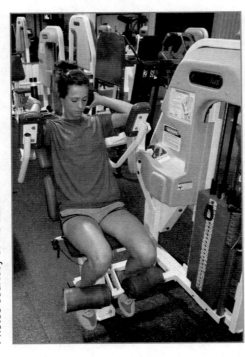

Reverse Crunch (Isolation)

**Major Muscles Involved

    1. Abdominal (lower rectus abdominus)

**Execution

    1. Lie with back on floor, lower legs held parallel to the floor, upper legs perpendicular to the floor.

    2. Arms are crossed across the chest with elbows pointing up.

    3. Keep head and shoulders on floor throughout movement.

    4. Using lower abdominal, lift hips off floor and bring knees to elbows.

    5. Lower legs to starting position.

 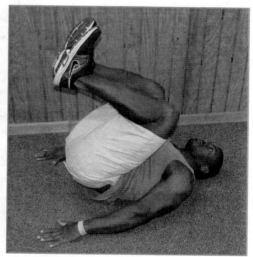

Photos courtesy of John Clark.

Hyperextension (Isolation)

**Major Muscles Involved

    1. Lower back

    2. Buttocks

**Execution

    1. Use a hyperextension bench made specifically for this exercise.

    2. Hips are placed across pad; lower legs at heels are hooked under restraining pad.

    3. Chest is facing floor; arms can be crossed across chest or hands held behind head.

    4. Upper torso should be lowered perpendicular to the floor.

    5. Using lower back and buttocks muscles, slowly raise torso upward to a position parallel to the floor.

Plank

**Major Muscles Involved

1. Rectus Abdominis

**Execution

1. Lay prone on the ground.
2. With your body straight, balance your body on elbows and toes.
3. Hold in this position.
4. Dynamic planks can be accomplished with moving hands and legs while maintaining balance.

Straight Leg Deadlift (Basic)

**Major Muscles Involved

1. Hamstrings
2. Buttocks
3. Lower back

**Execution

1. Use a barbell or dumbbells.
2. Stand on a low box or block of wood (normally 8–15" high).
3. Grasp the barbell with an overhand grip, hands shoulder-width.
4. Stand erect, feet shoulder-width.
5. Bar will rest at top of thighs.
6. "Stand at attention" and hold this posture throughout the movement.
7. Bend forward keeping the legs straight, <u>back flat</u>, shoulders back, head up.
8. Bar should be lowered as far as flexibility will allow.
9. Slowly reverse direction to starting position.
10. Do not lean back at top of movement.

Photos courtesy of John Clark.

Deadlift (Basic)

**Major Muscles Involved

1. Lower back
2. Buttocks
3. Thighs
4. Upper back

**Execution

1. Begin with a barbell lying on floor.
2. Grasp bar with one hand in an underhand grip, the other hand using an overhand grip.
3. Feet are flat on floor, shoulder-width, toes pointed straight ahead, shins touching bar.
4. Arms stay straight throughout movement.
5. Keeping a flat back, dip hips to a position lower than the shoulders, but higher than the knees.
6. Lift the barbell from the floor by straightening the legs. The back stays flat, arms straight. The bar will rest across upper thighs.
7. Slowly return to starting position.

Photos courtesy of John Clark.

STRENGTH TRAINING FOR LIFE

COMPONENTS OF WELLNESS

Overall wellness is important in order to have a successful weight training program. The overall goal of wellness is not just physical fitness, but the fulfillment of several dimensions. The concept of wellness includes five distinct components (Figure 10.1). Social health addresses the development and maintenance of personal relationships, establishing a network of family and friends, and having feelings of comfort in social settings. One example of strong social ties is meeting a new workout partner. A good workout partner is important to make sure lifts are done safely and properly.

The foundation of strong emotional health depends on stress management and the appropriate expression of our feelings. Although it is very normal to experience some highs and lows, the avoidance of drastic swings in emotions is important to mental health. A good strength training program can be an excellent outlet for dealing with the everyday stressors in life.

Spiritual health can mean different things to different people. Regardless of religious feelings or beliefs, spiritual health is a function of personal values. Having a true sense of purpose and direction in life, understanding human nature, maintaining sensitivity and respect for others, and having appreciation for the beauty of life are all a part of sound spiritual health.

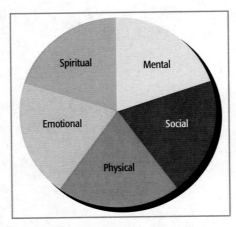

Figure 10.1 Components of Wellness (From *Fitness for Living* by Bill Hyman, Gary Oden, David Bacharach, and Tim Sebesta. Copyright © 2011 by Kendall Hunt Publishing Company. Reprinted by permission.)

Intellectual health addresses the mind and a perpetual love of learning. Reading, interacting with others, and attending lectures are all excellent methods to maintain intellectual health. Weight lifting is a great outlet for maintaining intellectual health because lifters desire additional knowledge to complement their exercise program.

Physical health involves taking good care of the body and its systems to ensure that they remain disease free and capable of functioning at a high level of efficiency. As we have suggested throughout this text, physical health contributes significantly to total health and well-being. A comprehensive weight training program improves muscular strength and endurance as well as body composition, cardiovascular endurance through circuit training, and flexibility. Even though a comprehensive weight training program can meet many of the health-related components of fitness, it is important to get involved in a wide variety of activities to improve physical fitness. A good cardiovascular endurance program along with circuit weight training can quickly improve body composition by reducing body fat at a faster rate. Physical health has perhaps the most widespread impact on overall health and can be accomplished in so many different ways. Improved quality of life and a longer life are the common end results, making it difficult to dispute the advantages of physical activity.

HEALTH BENEFITS OF PHYSICAL ACTIVITY

There is a great deal of conflicting information in regards to understanding health and wellness. The 20th century brought about tremendous advances in the understanding of health and wellness, not only through advances in the medical field but in a more thorough understanding of how our lifestyles impact our health status. Even though many of our daily tasks are now automated, it is still important to make time to exercise to improve our overall health. Risks to our society have turned from infectious diseases (polio, rubella, tuberculosis, influenza, etc.) to chronic diseases (obesity, hypertension, heart disease, stroke, cancer, emphysema, etc.). This transition took the better part of the century, and only in the last few decades have we begun to recognize the relationship between physical activity and mortality. The major risk factors for our top killers (cardiovascular disease and cancer) are related to a sedentary lifestyle. Exercising, proper nutrition and not smoking are three of the most important areas to focus on to reduce our risk for chronic diseases. Being healthy and physically fit is a personal choice. All of our daily choices impact our health. The "Be Active Your Way" program has a website that you might find useful. It includes a 14-page document provided by the government, with four components from getting started to being active for life: http://www.health. gov/paguidelines/pdf/adultguide.pdf. Among the benefits are risk reductions in diabetes, hypertension, heart disease, stroke, and colon cancer.

FACTORS IMPORTANT FOR HEALTH AND LONGEVITY

Physical activity by itself cannot guarantee good health—other factors undoubtedly contribute to overall health. However, numerous research studies have shown that higher levels of physical activity are associated with decreased risks of coronary heart disease, cerebrovascular disease, hypertension, osteoporosis, Type 2 diabetes mellitus, colon cancer, and possibly breast cancer. The American College of Sports Medicine (ACSM) has initiated a program entitled Exercise is Medicine; the program is worldwide, and the basic recommendations are straightforward.

Do moderately intense cardio 30 minutes/day, 5 days/per week

OR

Do vigorously intense cardio 20 minutes/day, 3 days/per week

AND

Do 8–10 strength-training exercises, 8–12 repetitions of each exercise twice each week.

Moderate-intensity physical activity means working hard enough to raise your heart rate and break a sweat, yet still being able to carry on a conversation. It should be noted that to lose weight or maintain weight loss, 60 to 90 minutes of physical activity may be necessary. The 30-minute recommendation is for the average healthy adult to maintain health and reduce the risk for chronic disease, not to use to lose unwanted fat mass. Encouraging everyone to do 20–30 minutes or more of vigorous physical activity every day parallels the Surgeon General's Report, which indicates that a minimum caloric expenditure of 1,000 weight-adjusted calories per week reduces the risk of most chronic diseases and premature death.

No single factor has been shown to influence health more than physical activity.

MOTIVATIONAL TECHNIQUES

The key to motivating yourself is to make sure you enjoy what you are doing and make the necessary time to exercise. Do not "find" time to exercise! "Make" time to exercise, as this makes it a priority in your life. Finding time instead of making time to exercise is like finding an item for someone else as opposed to trying to find something you personally lost. You will make time to find whatever you lost but will many times find time to seek something someone else lost. Activities must deliver a level of enjoyment in order to persevere. Allow your exercise time to also be a social time, enjoying various activities with family and friends. Enjoyment provides the best motivation for a lifetime of activity.

Once activity becomes a daily routine, it will be hard for you to imagine life without it and what it was like when you did not exercise. But prior to that time, you must consider activity a priority. This will help you continue a good habit. We hope that this book has encouraged you to develop a successful weight training program and also to seek a healthy and active lifestyle. It's great to be fit, and to know that a great weight training program in addition to a healthy lifestyle will definitely improve your overall quality of life.

PLANNING YOUR FITNESS PROGRAM

Please complete the wellness lifestyle questionnaire at the end of this chapter. Based upon your results, begin to create goals, followed by strategies for maintaining and/or improving your status in each area.

chapter 10
LABORATORY   10.1

Personal Health Profile

Think about your overall health status and specific health behaviors and respond to each item below:

	Column A Yes	Column B No
1. Engage in vigorous exercise (running, swimming, brisk walking, aerobics, a related activity) for 20–30 minutes 3 to 5 days per week.		
2. Perform resistance exercises to strengthen my bones and muscles.		
3. Always warm-up and cool-down before and after exercise.		
4. Get 7–8 hours of sleep each night.		
5. Know the warning signs for cancer, heart attack, and stroke.		
6. See my doctor regularly for checkups.		
7. Know the appropriate self-examinations and perform them regularly.		
8. Body weight is within the recommended healthy range.		
9. Consistently choose low-fat, high fiber foods.		
10. Consume salt and sugar in moderation.		
11. Eat lots of fruits and vegetables.		
12. Have never used tobacco.		
13. Socialize with close friends weekly.		
14. Always wear my seatbelt.		
15. Drive carefully, within the speed limit, and take no unnecessary risks while driving.		

From *Fitness for Living* by Bill Hyman, Gary Oden, David Bacharach, and Tim Sebesta. Copyright © 2011 by Kendall Hunt Publishing Company. Reprinted by permission.

	Column A *Yes*	Column B *No*
16. Abstain from alcohol or drink lightly (no more than1 drink per day forwomen, no more than 2 drinks per day for men).	_____	_____
17. Never drink and drive or ride with a driver who has been drinking.	_____	_____
18. Have several stress management and coping strategies that I use successfully.	_____	_____
19. Know my blood pressure and it is within the desirable range.	_____	_____
20. Know my cholesterol level and it is within the desirable range.	_____	_____
21. Have good study habits.	_____	_____
22. Have several leisure time activities which I enjoy.	_____	_____
23. Get tired easily.	_____	_____
24. Get very little or no exercise.	_____	_____
25. Eat out often.	_____	_____
26. Consume a diet high in cholesterol and fat.	_____	_____
27. Smoke cigarettes.	_____	_____
28. 28. Use other forms of tobacco.	_____	_____
29. Waste time watching television, sleeping too much, or being idle.	_____	_____
30. Drink to intoxication.	_____	_____
31. Feel l'ife is highly stressful.	_____	_____
32. Frequently feel overwhelmed with too many tasks and expectations.	_____	_____
33. Don't eat breakfast or skip other meals regularly.	_____	_____
34. Do not limit the time that I am exposed to the sun and rarely wear sunscreen.	_____	_____

Add up every check mark made in column A and multiply by 3. Determine your relative risk by identifying your health behavior score in one of the categories below:

Your Score	Grade	Comment
90–100	A	Overall excellent health practices. Few risky behaviors. Nice work.
80–89	B	Good health behaviors. Where could improvements be made?
70–79	C	OK in most areas, but can definitely improve in others.
60–69	D	Need some help in reducing health risks.
Below 60	F	Have few healthy behaviors. Immediate action is needed.

STRENGTH TRAINING FOR ALL POPULATIONS

CHILDREN AND WEIGHT TRAINING

Generally, children have been raised to be active and energetic. Years ago children were encouraged to go outside and "play until the street lights go on." However, society has changed that model and perspective; therefore, children are now not as active before, during, and after school. Family situations and academic budget cutbacks have changed the activity level of children. Today, children are becoming more obese and less active than they were several decades ago (Anderson & Butcher, 2006).

Because youth sports have become more commonplace and competitive in recent years, coaches and parents are looking for different methods and opportunities to help young athletes improve their performance. Resistance exercise programs can assist in offering the young athlete a competitive advantage; however, concerns continue to remain as to the safety and effectiveness of these programs. A sensible strength-training program requires a time commitment of perhaps less than one hour per session, three times per week in order to produce significant results.

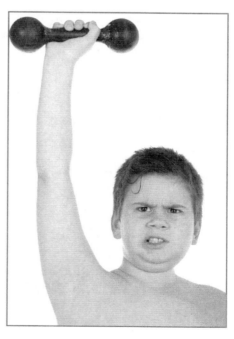

© Zametalov, 2013. Used under license from Shutterstock, Inc.

When instructing children regarding a weight training program, the primary concern should focus on safety and discipline in the weight room. Often children will view a weight room as an opportunity for recreation, so care must be used with implementing discipline in these children. Children need to be mature enough to handle the repetitive nature of a resistance exercise program, as the "newness" of physical training could wear off quickly. This can lead to a less-disciplined atmosphere in the weight room, unfortunately leading to detrimental effects; therefore, children should be supervised at all times during their weight training sessions.

Certainly the growing bones of a child are more susceptible to certain types of injury than those of an adult, primarily because of the presence of cartilage (Micheli, 1984). An appropriately designed strength training program has been shown to be safer in preadolescents and adolescents than other sporting activities (Hamill, 1994). Also, a broad-based training program that includes resistance exercise has been shown to reduce sports related injuries in adolescents (Faigenbaum & Schram, 2004). Children as young as age 6 have been shown to improve strength when following proper guidelines (Falk & Mor, 1996). There is, however, considerable discussion as to what constitutes the word "proper." Emphasis should be placed on correct technique and safety as opposed to number of lifts and amount of weight lifted. The American College of Sports Medicine specifically states that children should exercise with a resistance that will allow them to perform no fewer than eight repetitions. Research supports the contention that a higher repetition-moderate load resistance program should be utilized during the initial adaptation period for children (Faigenbaum, Westcott, Loud & Long, 1999). However, children who were properly supervised during maximal lifting showed no injuries, indicating that even maximum intensity training can be safe for children when adequate supervision is present (Faigenbaum, Westcott, Long, Loud, Delmonico & Micheli, (1998). Most aspiring young weight trainers should strive to build muscles with higher repetitions and lighter resistance in order to reduce the risk of injury and to learn the proper technique for each exercise performed.

One of the goals of this textbook is to provide the student (both young and old) with a solid, comprehensive resistance exercise program that will lead to a lifelong commitment to a regular exercise program. Explosive type lifts, such as the power clean, should be avoided as these exercises place a large strain on vulnerable areas of the body. Research has shown that the lower back area (even in children) is most susceptible to increased risk of injury due to explosive type lifts (Brown & Kimball, 1983). While other training methods may be touted in the literature (plyometrics, boot camps, and others), care should be utilized when beginning these types of programs, especially in the initial stages of an individual's workout career.

ELDERLY AND WEIGHT TRAINING

Current research on the elderly participating in a strength training program has produced some remarkable findings (Tannenbaum & Mayo, 2003), as a great deal of research has focused on the impact of strength training for elderly individuals. Sedentary older adults can achieve excellent strength results with a coordinated strength and resistance program (Misic, Valentine, Rosengren, Woods & Evans, 2008). Individuals with knee pain discovered that a strength training program significantly reduced their pain and stiffness and improved other aspects of their physical function (Thomas, Muir, Doherty, Jones, O'Reilly & Bassey, 2002). Older populations exhibit greater predisposition to degenerative musculoskeletal conditions, increasing the importance of a well-rounded fitness regimen. Well-conditioned muscles can increase physical capacity (thereby allowing continuation of activity), reduce the risk of injury, and help improve personal appearance. Also, weight training has been shown to decrease an individual's risk of osteoporosis and reduce the signs of other diseases including arthritis and type 2 diabetes (Seguin & Nelson, 2003).

Sarcopenia (muscle loss) generally begins around age 45 when muscle mass can decline at a rate of approximately 1 percent per year (Janssen, Heymsfield, Wang & Ross, 2000). Muscle strength, or the ability to exert force, is directly related to the amount of muscle mass in the body. As muscle mass decreases, so does muscle strength. Continuing, as strength decreases, so does physical functioning including such activities as the ability to climb stairs, perform chores, dance, walk, etc. The risk of falling is certainly

© ollyy, 2013. Used under license from Shutterstock, Inc.

a concern of the elderly, and risk increases with a corresponding decrease in strength (Bucher, 1997). Muscle loss will occur in people of all fitness levels, even accomplished older athletes. No one can completely halt sarcopenia; however, a well-balanced resistance-exercise program can decrease it dramatically.

GENDER DIFFERENCES

Males traditionally tend to have more muscle mass than women, therefore men will respond to a resistance program quicker. However, men and women can gain strength at the same rate, with differences being apparent in absolute numbers—men generally have more overall weight and therefore have greater potential of "buildable" muscle.

Often women will stay away from resistance exercise programs due to the mistaken belief that they will dramatically increase their muscle size. However, women will generally not develop large muscles from weight training due to the lack of testosterone production in most women. Because testosterone is a growth-type hormone, the differences in muscle mass is more prevalent in males. Testosterone levels are generally much higher in males

© Aleksandr Markin, 2013. Used under license from Shutterstock, Inc.

than those in females, leading to the increased ability of males to add lean tissue. Most women can achieve excellent results with a well-designed fitness program, leading to loss of body fat and improved muscle tone.

Different and potentially serious medical conditions are often present in individuals of all ages. Most conditions are relatively benign; however, some can be very serious in nature. Exercise is often utilized as a method to treat certain medical conditions; however, some activity programs are not beneficial for every condition. Resistance exercise has been shown to offer some benefits for several of the following conditions. All preexisting medical conditions should be checked by a physician in order to determine if resistance exercise is contraindicated or not suited for their individual situation.

HYPERTENSION

Hypertension or prehypertension affects approximately 57 percent of the American adult population (Ostchega, Yoon & Hughes, 2008). Because hypertension is a risk factor for stroke, concern is warranted in individuals with this condition. To complicate matters, resistance exercise has shown to cause dramatic increases in both systolic and diastolic blood pressure in lifters (McDougall, McKelvie & Moroz, 1958)

However, with proper precautions, resistance exercise can be an integral part of an exercise program for individuals with hypertension. Maximal lifts should be avoided, focusing on repetitions with 30–40 percent of IRM for upper body and 50–60 percent I RM for lower body. Because blood pressure responds to increased repetitions, sets to failure should be avoided. Rest over 90 seconds after each set is recommended. Finally, breathing patterns should be monitored as breath holding can lead to the Valsalva maneuver, thereby dramatically increasing blood pressure.

If the initial resting blood pressure is 180/110 mm HG or higher, resistance exercise should be avoided (Sorace, Churila & Magyari, 2012). All individuals with hypertension should consult their physicians before beginning an exercise program, particularly one that includes a resistance exercise component.

DIABETES

It is well documented that physical activity in general is important in the management of type 2 diabetes. The reduction of adipose tissue is of primary importance in decreasing insulin resistance in the body. Aerobic exercise is generally considered the preferred modality for increasing physical activity in these patients. However, it is apparent that the muscle contraction process increases glucose uptake in the skeletal muscle (Holloszy & Hansen, 1996). Resistance

Scenario:

Helen, a 24-year-old college student, would like to begin to weight train, but her friends tell her that any weight training will give her big muscles. What advice can you give to Helen?

exercise does offer an alternative to aerobic exercise for improving glucose control in individuals with diabetes (Fenicchia, Kanaley, Azevedo, Miller, Weistock, Carhart & Ploutz-Snyder, 2004).

Studies indicate that a combination of aerobic and resistance exercise can have the greatest effect in controlling type 2 diabetes (Sigal, et al., 2007).

CARDIOVASCULAR DISEASE AND REHABILITATION

Resistance training has been associated with increased skeletal muscle and increased function. However, resistance training alone is shown to have a limited effect on cardiovascular disease risk factors (Braith & Stewart, 2006). Therefore, a solid recommendation would be to combine resistance exercise with aerobic exercise in order to have a greater effect on reducing risk of cardiovascular disease.

Aerobic exercise has also been indicated as the primary form of exercise rehabilitation with individuals suffering from congestive heart failure (CHF). Research has shown that resistance exercise with individuals with CHF can increase both strength and endurance, thereby indicating that a proper resistance program is both safe and recommended for these individuals (Hare, et al., 1999).

Exercise has long been utilized as a major component in cardiac rehabilitation programs. Generally, traditional aerobic activities are utilized, including walking, cycling, or swimming. However, the effectiveness of a weight training program in cardiac rehabilitation has been shown to assist patients with their rehabilitation. Circuit weight training, or moving from each resistance exercise quickly to the next, appears to be safe and can also result in significant increases in aerobic endurance and strength (Kelemen, et al., 1986).

Anatomy

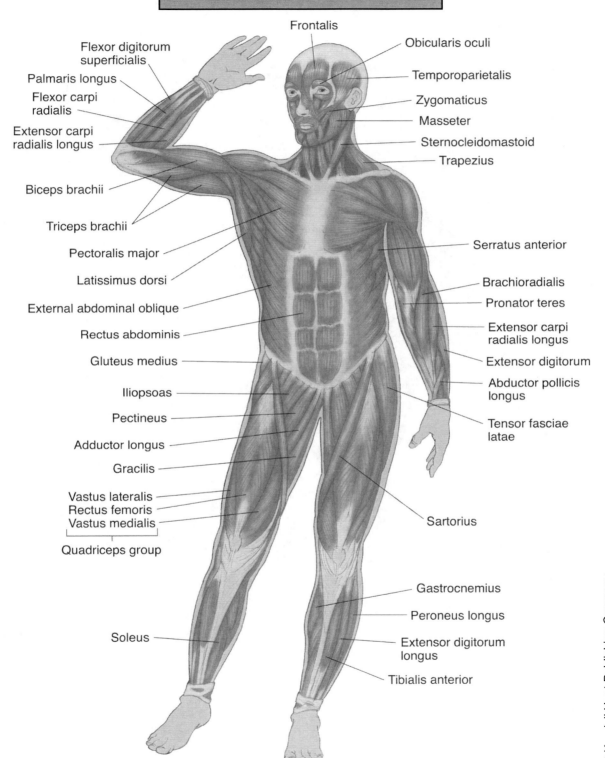

Frontalis

Flexor digitorum superficialis

Palmaris longus

Flexor carpi radialis

Extensor carpi radialis longus

Biceps brachii

Triceps brachii

Pectoralis major

Latissimus dorsi

External abdominal oblique

Rectus abdominis

Gluteus medius

Iliopsoas

Pectineus

Adductor longus

Gracilis

Vastus lateralis
Rectus femoris
Vastus medialis
Quadriceps group

Soleus

Obicularis oculi

Temporoparietalis

Zygomaticus

Masseter

Sternocleidomastoid

Trapezius

Serratus anterior

Brachioradialis

Pronator teres

Extensor carpi radialis longus

Extensor digitorum

Abductor pollicis longus

Tensor fasciae latae

Sartorius

Gastrocnemius

Peroneus longus

Extensor digitorum longus

Tibialis anterior

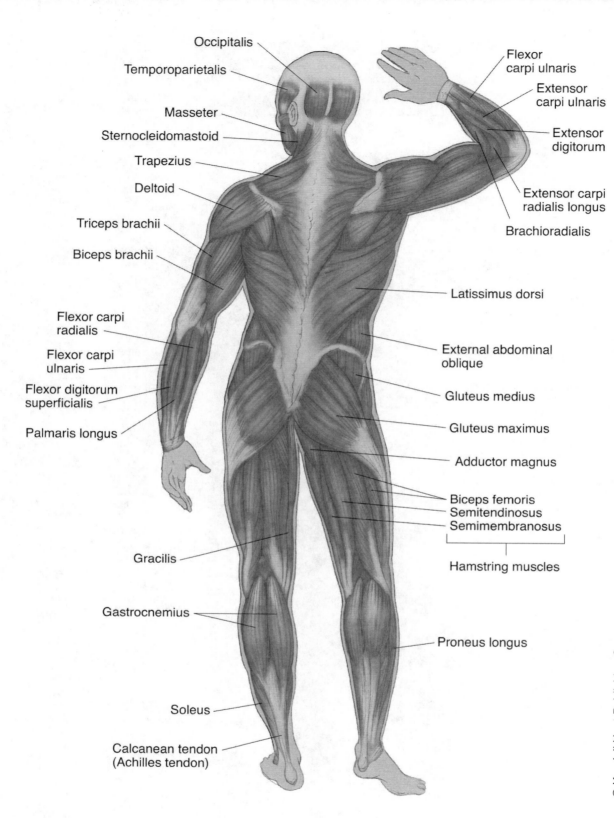

Occipitalis

Temporoparietalis

Masseter

Sternocleidomastoid

Trapezius

Deltoid

Triceps brachii

Biceps brachii

Flexor carpi radialis

Flexor carpi ulnaris

Flexor digitorum superficialis

Palmaris longus

Gracilis

Gastrocnemius

Soleus

Calcanean tendon (Achilles tendon)

Flexor carpi ulnaris

Extensor carpi ulnaris

Extensor digitorum

Extensor carpi radialis longus

Brachioradialis

Latissimus dorsi

External abdominal oblique

Gluteus medius

Gluteus maximus

Adductor magnus

Biceps femoris
Semitendinosus
Semimembranosus

Hamstring muscles

Proneus longus

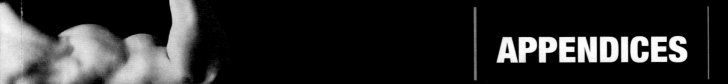

APPENDIX A: WORKOUT LOG

DATE:	SET 1		SET 2		SET 3		SET 4	
EXERCISE	Rep	Wt	Rep	Wt	Rep	Wt	Rep	Wt

DATE:	SET 1		SET 2		SET 3		SET 4	
EXERCISE	Rep	Wt	Rep	Wt	Rep	Wt	Rep	Wt

DATE:	SET 1		SET 2		SET 3		SET 4	
EXERCISE	Rep	Wt	Rep	Wt	Rep	Wt	Rep	Wt

From *Fundamentals of Weight Training* by Matthew C. Wagner, William E. Nix, and Gary L. Oden. Copyright © 2011 by Kendall Hunt Publishing Company. Reprinted by permission.

DATE:	SET 1		SET 2		SET 3		SET 4	
EXERCISE	Rep	Wt	Rep	Wt	Rep	Wt	Rep	Wt

DATE:	SET 1		SET 2		SET 3		SET 4	
EXERCISE	Rep	Wt	Rep	Wt	Rep	Wt	Rep	Wt

DATE:	SET 1		SET 2		SET 3		SET 4	
EXERCISE	Rep	Wt	Rep	Wt	Rep	Wt	Rep	Wt

DATE:	SET 1		SET 2		SET 3		SET 4	
EXERCISE	Rep	Wt	Rep	Wt	Rep	Wt	Rep	Wt

DATE:		SET 1		SET 2		SET 3		SET 4	
EXERCISE		Rep	Wt	Rep	Wt	Rep	Wt	Rep	Wt

DATE:		SET 1		SET 2		SET 3		SET 4	
EXERCISE		Rep	Wt	Rep	Wt	Rep	Wt	Rep	Wt

DATE:		SET 1		SET 2		SET 3		SET 4	
EXERCISE		Rep	Wt	Rep	Wt	Rep	Wt	Rep	Wt

DATE:		SET 1		SET 2		SET 3		SET 4	
EXERCISE		Rep	Wt	Rep	Wt	Rep	Wt	Rep	Wt

DATE:		SET 1		SET 2		SET 3		SET 4	
EXERCISE		**Rep**	**Wt**	**Rep**	**Wt**	**Rep**	**Wt**	**Rep**	**Wt**

DATE:		SET 1		SET 2		SET 3		SET 4	
EXERCISE		**Rep**	**Wt**	**Rep**	**Wt**	**Rep**	**Wt**	**Rep**	**Wt**

DATE:		SET 1		SET 2		SET 3		SET 4	
EXERCISE		**Rep**	**Wt**	**Rep**	**Wt**	**Rep**	**Wt**	**Rep**	**Wt**

DATE:		SET 1		SET 2		SET 3		SET 4	
EXERCISE		**Rep**	**Wt**	**Rep**	**Wt**	**Rep**	**Wt**	**Rep**	**Wt**

DATE:	SET 1		SET 2		SET 3		SET 4	
EXERCISE	Rep	Wt	Rep	Wt	Rep	Wt	Rep	Wt

APPENDIX B: ANATOMY

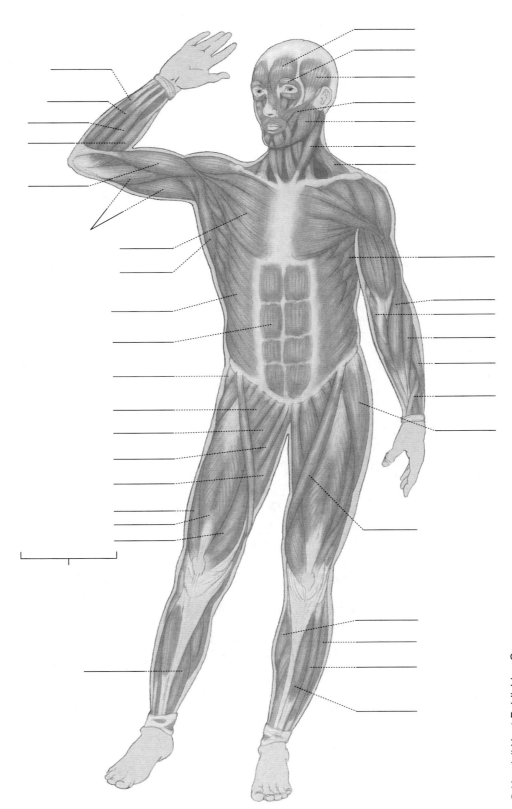

Anatomy

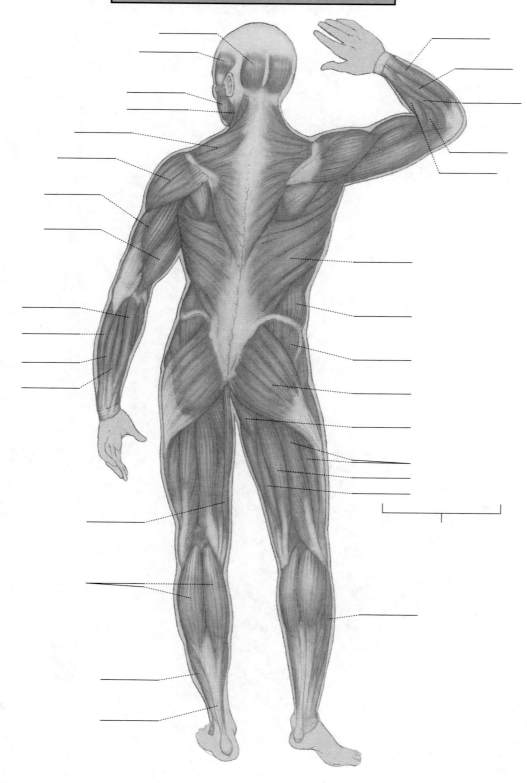

APPENDIX C: OBSERVATION REPORT 1

Name _____

Date _____

Place of observation:_____

Time of day: _____

What was the primary purpose of his/her exercise session?

How long did the session last?

What muscle groups did he/she focus on?

How many exercises did she/he perform? List different exercises.

How many sets of each exercise did she/he perform? List total amount of sets.

Did he/she utilize a spotter, collars, or other safety devices when necessary?

Rate her/his overall form from 1-10 on their resistance exercises.

Why did you assign him/her that rating?

What would be your two primary recommendations to this individual to increase the effectiveness of his/her workout?

APPENDIX C: OBSERVATION REPORT 2

Name _____

Date _____

Place of observation:_____

Time of day: _____

What was the primary purpose of his/her exercise session?

How long did the session last?

What muscle groups did he/she focus on?

How many exercises did she/he perform? List different exercises.

How many sets of each exercise did she/he perform? List total amount of sets.

Did he/she utilize a spotter, collars, or other safety devices when necessary?

Rate her/his overall form from 1-10 on their resistance exercises.

Why did you assign him/her that rating?

What would be your two primary recommendations to this individual to increase the effectiveness of his/her workout?

Abduction: Movement of a limb away from the midline of the body

Acceleration: An increase in velocity

Actin: One of the two primary contractile myofilaments; binds with myosin to cause muscle action

Adduction: Movement of a limb toward the midline of the body

Adenosine triphosphate (ATP): The universal energy-carrying molecule manufactured in all living cells as a means of capturing and storing energy

Agonist: The muscle contracting or performing work

Alternated grip: A grip in which one hand is pronated and the other hand is supinated

Anabolic: Referring to the synthesis of larger molecules from smaller molecules

Antagonist: The muscle opposing the contraction, or resisting the work

Anthropometry: The science of measurement applied to the human body; generally includes measurements of height, weight, and selected body girths.

Appendicular skeleton: Skeletal subdivision that consists of the shoulder girdle, arms, legs, and pelvis

Assumption of risk: A defense for the personal trainer whereby the client knows that there are inherent risks with the participation in an activity but still voluntarily decides to participate

Atrophy: Loss of size, or wasting of part of the body

Automated external defibrillator (AED): Portable device that identifies heart rhythms; uses audio or visual prompts, or both, to direct the correct response; and delivers the appropriate shock only when needed.

Axial skeleton: Skeletal subdivision that consists of the skull, vertebral column, and thorax (rib cage)

Barbell: Steel bars 3–7 feet long on which circular iron plates of known weight are placed. The bar may be straight or a bent EZ curl bar.

Basic exercise: An exercise that works one or more large muscle groups in conjunction with other, smaller muscle groups. Basic exercises are used for building muscle mass. Low repetitions and heavy weights are the norm.

Body building: A sport or activity in which the primary objective is to develop the size of skeletal muscles. Bodybuilders focus on building muscles proportionally (symmetrically), minimizing body fat, and increasing muscle strength. The main objective of bodybuilders is on muscular development, not strength.

Body composition: Percentages of fat, bone, and muscle in the human body

Body part sequencing: Muscles should be worked in order from the largest in mass down to the smallest. Large muscle groups require much greater energy expenditure to train than do smaller muscle groups.

Body weight exercises: Resistance training in which the individual used his/her own body weight as the form of resistance

Carbohydrate: Abbreviated CHO. Primary fuel (nutrition) that provides energy in the body

Catabolic: Breakdown of larger molecules into smaller molecules

Cheating: A lift executed with the addition of muscle groups other than the prime movers

Circuit training: Form of weight training involving moving from one exercise to another in a rapid fashion

Closed grip: Grip in which the thumb is wrapped around the bar so that the bar is fully held in the palm of the hand

Closed kinetic chain: Movement during which the most distal body part's motion is significantly restricted or fixed; often occurs with lower (or upper) body movements with the feet (or hands) on the floor. Involves co-contraction of the agonist/antagonist muscle group.

Collar: Safety device fitted over the ends of a barbell or dumbbell to keep weights from sliding toward the end of the bar

Concentric: Raising the weight or resistance, also known as positive work

Contraindication: Activity or practice that is inadvisable or prohibited because of a given injury

Core exercise: Exercises that involve movement at two or more primary joints and recruit one or more large muscle groups or areas

Core muscles: Specifically referring to the rectus abdominus, the erector spinae, and the external and internal obliques

Cross-bridges: Projections around the myosin filament that latch onto the binding site on actin

Delayed-onset muscle soreness (DOMS): Muscle discomfort or pain that occurs 24 to 48 hours after a heavy bout of exercise

Detraining: Reversal of the adaptations stimulated by training. The effects of detraining can occur very rapidly when work loads are significantly reduced.

Dumbbell: A short barbell, 12–16 inches in length, with fixed or removable weight plates

Duration: Measure of length of time an exercise session lasts

Eccentric: Lowering the weight or resistance, also known as negative work

Endurance: Ability of a muscle to repeatedly contract over time. The opposite of endurance is fatigue.

Ergogenic aid: Any substance, equipment, or program designed to improve human performance

Estrogen: Primary female hormone

Extension: Straightening out of a limb or joint, or lengthening of a joint angle

False grip: Grip where the thumb is not wrapped around the bar but instead is placed next to the index finger

Fat: Adipose tissue, vital for long term energy and insulation in the body

Fatigue: General sense of tiredness that is often accompanied by a decrease in muscular performance

Flexibility: Range of motion; movement of a body part from its anatomical position to its extreme limit. Flexibility is a component of fitness.

Flexion: Bending of a limb or joint, or shortening of a joint angle

Form: Technical skills employed to perform an activity. Synonymous with technique.

Force: Mechanical action applied to a body that tends to produce acceleration

Forced repetitions: Resistance exercise movements that are successfully completed with assistance from a spotter

Frequency: Number of times workout sessions are conducted. The quality of the work performed is more important than the frequency.

Frontal plane: Vertical plane that divides the body or organs into front and back portions

Fully extended: Refers to an appendage (arms, legs). Recommendation is to always have a joint slightly flexed and to never lock out or attempt to fully extend a joint during an exercise.

Gender differences: Basic difference between male and females participating in an exercise program. Often a function of the endocrine system.

General warm up: Type of warm up that involves performing basic activities requiring movement of the major muscle groups (e. g., jogging, cycling, or jumping rope)

Gloves: Safety/comfort device worn by weight trainers over the hands to strengthen grip and reduce friction during training

Golgi tendon organ: Sensory receptor that monitors tension and is located in the muscle tendon

Grip width: Distance between the hands when placed on a bar

Hyperplasia: Increase in the number of muscle fibers

Hyperextension: Continued extension past normal range of motion. Not all limbs have ability to hyperextend.

Hypertrophy: Increase in size of tissue or cells

Indication: Activity that will benefit an injured client

Informed consent: Protective legal document that informs the client of any inherent risks associated with fitness testing and participation in an exercise program

Intensity: Quality of work performed. The degree of effort expended during a lift or exercise.

Isokinetic: Type of exercise where the force is applied at a constant velocity – "Same speed"

Isolation exercise: Exercise that stresses a single muscle or muscle complex in relative isolation from the rest of the body. Isolation exercises are used more for shaping and defining each muscle or muscle group, utilizing higher repetitions and lighter weights.

Isometric: Type of exercise where force is applied with no change in the length of the muscle – no concentric or eccentric work occurs – "Same length"

Isotonic: Type of exercise utilizing resistance, such as dumbbells or most weight machines – "same resistance"

Joint: Articulation; where two or more bones come together

Kettlebell: Large iron ball or resistance connected to a handle

Kinematics: Description of motion with respect to space and time, and without regard to the forces or torques involved

Kinetics: Assessment of motion with regard to forces and force-related measures

Liftoff: Movement of the bar from the supports of a bench or rack to a position in which the lifter can begin the exercise

Ligaments: Soft tissue that attaches a bone to another bone

Load: Amount of weight assigned to an exercise set

Lockout: Full extension of a joint at the end of a range of motion

Maximal heart rate (MHR): Actual limit of myocardial contractions that can be attained in one minute

Mechanical advantage: ratio of the length of the movement arm through which a muscular force acts to the length of movement arm through which a resistive force acts

Medicine ball: Heavy, spherical, filled object usually weighing between 1 to 20 pounds and made of leather, rubber or plastic

Mesocycle: Division of a periodized program that lasts several weeks to a few months

Microcycle: Division of a periodized program that lasts from one to four weeks and can include daily and weekly training variations

Mode: Specific type of exercise or activity that will be performed during an exercise session

Momentum: Property of a moving body that is determined by the product of its mass and velocity

Motivation: Psychological construct that influences behavior, commitment, attitude, and the desire to exercise

Motor unit: Motor neuron and all the muscle fiber it innervates

Muscle fiber: Structural unit of muscle. Also referred to as a muscle cell.

Muscle spindle: Sensory organ within muscle fibers that relays sensory information about lengthened speed of stretch to the central nervous system

Muscular endurance training: Resistance training program designed to target the ability of a muscle or muscle group to contract repeatedly over an extended time period. Also called strength endurance training.

Muscular endurance: Ability of the neuromuscular system to produce force in a repetitive manner

Negligence: Failure to conform one's conduct to a generally accepted standard or the failure to act as a reasonably prudent person would act under the circumstances

Neutral grip: Hand position on a bar in which the palm faces in and the knuckles point out to the side (as in a handshake)

Olympic lifting: Refers to the Olympic sport of Weightlifting, which tests strength and power through two methods of lifting a barbell overhead—the Snatch and the Clean and Jerk

One repetition maximum (1RM): The highest amount of weight an individual can lift for a single repetition of a particular exercise

Open grip: *See false grip.*

Osteoporosis: Pathological state of osteopenia in which bones become porous and brittle resulting in increased disposition for fractures

Overhand grip: Hand position on a bar in which the hand grasps the bar with the palm down and the knuckles up

Overtraining: Inability to recover after exercise - Occurs by performing too many sets per body part, by exceeding 60-minute training sessions, or by pushing the body past its ability to recuperate between workouts.

PAR-Q (Physical Activity Readiness Questionnaire): Assessment tool to initially screen apparently healthy clients who want to engage in low-intensity exercise and identify clients who require additional medical screening

Periodization: Method of alternating or dividing training cycles so as to optimize training efficiency

Plank: An isometric used to improve core strength and stability. Utilizes a prone position with only elbows and toes touching the ground.

Plateau: Cessation of gains in the conditioning program as a result of improper training techniques or lack of variety of the exercise program.

Power: A combination of two factors: movement speed and movement force. Increasing movement speed or increasing movement force, or increasing both, will improve performance power.

Power lifting: Sport conceived as a pure test of strength. Consists of three events: squat, bench press, and dead lift.

Progression: Gradual and consistent increase in the intensity of an exercise program

Progressive overload principle: Basis of all exercise programs is that strength, endurance, and muscle-size increase, within limits, in response to repetitive exercise against progressively increased resistance

Prone: Body position facedown

Pronation: Type of grip utilized by lifters involving the palm of the hand facing away from the lifter

Proprioceptors: Sensory receptors in the muscle (Golgi tendon organs and muscle spindles) that are sensitive and respond to changes in the muscle, either load or tension

Protein: Series of amino acids, combines with water to make up muscle tissue. Essential nutrient for muscle growth.

Recruitment: Process in which tasks that require more force involve the activation of more motor units

Repetition: Continuation and duplication of identical movements. The same movement is repeated "X" number of times.

Resistance: Amount of weight or opposition utilized during an exercise

Resistance training: Opposition to muscles supplied by weights, machines, resistance bands, and any number of other devices that resist movement of the exerciser

Rest interval: Time period between two sets

Risk stratification: Method to initially classify clients as being at low, moderate, or high possibility for coronary, peripheral vascular, or metabolic disease

Sarcopenia: Loss of muscle tissue due to aging process. Generally begins around age 45 when muscle mass begins to decline at a rate of approximately 1 percent per year.

Set: Completion of a predetermined number of repetitions. The "X" number of repetitions of the same movement constitutes one set. Examples: 3 × 20 (3 sets of 20 repetitions in each set) 4 × 10 (4 sets of 10 repetitions in each set)

Single-joint exercise: Resistance activity involving movement at only one primary articulation

Smith machine: Specific type of exercise machine including a free-weight barbell moving along a guide rod or tack, thereby decreasing the resistance and restricting motion

Specificity: Strategy to train a client in a certain way to produce a particular change or result

Split routine: Exercise routine in which different muscle groups are trained on different days or training sessions

Spot reducing: Attempting to eliminate fat in a specific part of the body, such as the abdomen, legs, or hips. There is no evidence that spot reducing is possible.

Spotting: Safety technique utilized by the presence of another lifter to monitor the lift and assist the lifter as needed. A spotter is a person who is in a position to help the lifter complete the lift if it becomes necessary.

Sticking point: Most difficult part of the exercise that typically occurs soon after the transition from the eccentric to the concentric phase

Strain: Injury (acute or chronic) to a muscle

Strength: Ability to exert force

Supination: Type of hand grip utilized by a weight lifter involving the palm of the hand facing toward the lifter

Technique: Synonymous with form

Tendons: Soft tissue that attaches a bone to a muscle in the body

Testosterone: Primary male hormone for building muscle mass

Torque: Tendency of a force to rotate an object about a fulcrum

Tropomyosin: Regulatory protein attached to actin that prevents actin from binding to the myosin cross-bridges

Troponin: Regulatory protein, attached to tropomyosin, that when activated shifts the tropomyosin to allow the actin to bind to the myosin cross-bridges

Type I muscle fiber: Type of muscle fiber characterized by slow rate of action and high fatigue resistance. Also known as slow twitch.

Type IIa muscle fiber: Type of muscle fiber characterized by a fast rate of action and relaxation, moderate aerobic and high glycolytic metabolic activity, and moderate fatigue resistance. Also known as a fast oxidative glycolytic fiber.

Type IIx muscle fiber: Type of muscle fiber characterized by a fast rate of action and relaxation, high glycolytic metabolic activity, and low fatigue resistance. Also known as a fast glycolytic fiber.

Valsalva phenomenon: Holding breath during the process of exertion. Compressing of the chest, thereby increasing intrathoracic pressure, leading to increased blood pressure. Not recommended during weight training.

Volume: Sum of all repetitions, sets, and resistance in a training session. The volume of the session does not necessarily relate to the intensity of the session.

Waiver: Contract that serves as evidence that the injured client waived his/her right to sue for negligence

Warm up: Important component of an exercise session to prepare the body physically and psychologically for upcoming tasks or events. A lower intensity exercise or demand.

Weight lifting: Weightlifting has a "generic" meaning that refers to the activity of lifting weights. However, it specifically refers to the Olympic sport of Weightlifting, which tests strength and power through two methods of lifting a barbell overhead— the Snatch and the Clean and Jerk.

Weight lifting belt: Strap or restraint system approximately 4 inches wide, used to support the abdomen and back and maintain proper spinal alignment during weight-lifting exercises

Weight trainer: Individual involved in weight training, resistance training, weightlifting, bodybuilding, or powerlifting

Weight training: Refers to any activity that involves the use of weights. The term weight training is commonly used to refer to people who lift weights but not for the purpose of competing in bodybuilding, power lifting, or weightlifting (although many people lift weights as a means for improving their performance in another sport).

Work: Product of the force exerted on an object and the distance the object moves. Mathematically expressed as force times distance.

Wrap: Joint support made of elastic bandages, neoprene, or leather

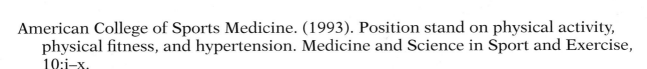

American College of Sports Medicine. (1993). Position stand on physical activity, physical fitness, and hypertension. Medicine and Science in Sport and Exercise, 10:i–x.

American Dietetic Association. Dietary supplements. http://www.eatright.org/Public/content. aspx?id=7918&terms=vitamin+supplement Accessed May 3, 2011.

Arnheim, D.D., and Prentice, W.E. (1993). Principles of Athletic Training (8th ed.) St. Louis: Mosby-Year Book, Inc.

Blair, S., Kohl, H., Paffenbarger, R., et al. (1989). Physical fitness and all causes of mortality: A prospective study of healthy men and women. Journal of Medical Association, 262:2395–2401.

Braith, R.W. and Stewart, K.J. (2006) Resistance exercise training: Its role in the prevention of cardiovascular disease. Circulation, 113: 2642–2650. Downloaded from http://circ.ahajournals.org/

Brown, E.W. and Kimball, R.G. (1983). Medical history associated with adolescent powerlifting. Pediatrics, 72, 636–644.

Bucher, D.M. (1997). Preserving mobility in older adults. Western Journal of Medicine, 167, 258–264.

Carnethon, M.R., Gidding, S.S., Nehgme, R., Sidney, S., Jacobs, D.R., and Liu, K. (2003). Cardiorespiratory fitness in young adulthood and the development of cardiovascular disease risk factors. Journal of the American Medical Association, 290, 3092–3100.

Centers for Disease Control and Prevention. (2004). Leading causes of death, 1900–1998. www.cdc.gov/nchs/statab/lead1900_1998.pdf

Coulston, A.M., and Boushey, C.]. (2008). Nutrition in the prevention and treatment of disease, 2nd edition. New York: Elsevier.

Faigenbaum, Kraemer, Cahill et al. (1996) Youth resistance training: Position statement paper and literature review. Strength and Conditioning 18 (6), 62–76.

Faigenbaum, A.L., Milliken, G. and Clourier et al., Perceived exertion during resistance exercise by children. Perceptual and Motor Skills, 98, 627–637.

Faigenbaum and Micheli. (1988). Youth strength training. Current comment from the American College of Sports Medicine. Sports Medicine Bulletin 32 (2), 28.

Faigenbaum, A.D., and Schram, J. (2004). Can resistance training reduce injuries in youth sports? Strength and conditioning Journal, 26 (3), 16–21.

Faigenbaum, A.D., Westcott, W.L., Long, C., Loud, R.L. Delmonico, M. and Micheli, L. (1998). Relationship between repetitions and selected percentage of the one repetition maximum in children. Pediatric Physical Therapy, 10 (3) 110–113.

Faigenbaum, A.D., Westcott, W.L., Loud, R.L. and Long, C. (1999). The effects of different resistance training protocols on muscular strength and endurance development in children. Pediatrics, 104(1) e5. http://pediatrics.aappublications.org/content/104/1/e5.full.html

Falk, B. and Mor, G. (1996). The effects of resistance and martial arts training in 6–8 year old boys. Pediatric Exercise Science, 8 (1), 48–56.

Fayolle-Minon, I. and Calmels, P. (2007). Effect of wearing a lumbar orthosis on trunk muscles: Study of the muscle strength after 21 days of use on healthy subjects. Joint Bone Spine, 75, 58–63.

Fenicchia, L.M., Kanaley, J.A., Azevedo, J.L., Miller, C.S., Weinstock, R.S., Carhart, R.L. and Ploutz-Snyder, L.L. (2004). Influence of resistance exercise training on glucose control in women with type 2 diabetes. Metabolism, 53 (3), 284–289.

Galvao, D.A., and Taaffe, D.R. (2005). Resistance exercise dosage in older adults: Single-versus multiset effects on physical performance and body composition. Journal of the American Geriatric Society, 53, 2090–2097.

Gettman, L.R., Ayres, J.J., Pollock, M.L. and Jackson, A.J. (1978). The effect of circuit weight training on strength, cardiorespiratory function, and body composition of adult men. Medicine and Science in Sports, 10 (3), 171–176.

Hamill, B.P. (1994). Relative safety of weightlifting and weight training. Journal of Strength and Conditioning Research, 8 (1), 53–57.

Hare, D.L., Ryan, T.M., Selig, S.E., Pellizzer, A.M., Wrigley, T.V. and Krum. H. (1999). Resistance exercise training increases muscle strength, endurance and blood flow in patients with chronic heart failure. American Journal of Cardiology, 83, 1674–1677.

Holloszy, J.O., and Hansen, P.A. (1997). Regulation of glucose transport into skeletal muscle. Reviews of Physiology, Biochemistry and Pharmacology. 128, 99–193.

Institute of Medicine of the National Academies (2010). Dietary Reference Intakes (DRIs): Recommended Dietary Allowances and Adequate Intakes. http://www.iom.edu/Activities/Nutrition/SummaryDRIs/~/media/Files/ActivityFiles/Nutrition/DRIs/RDAandAIs_VitaminandElements.pdf

Janssen, I., Heymsfield, S., Wang, Z., and Ross, R. (2000). Skeletal muscle mass and distribution in 468 men and women aged 18–88. Journal of Applied Physiology, 89, 81–88.

Jones, E.J., Richardson, P.A., Smith, M.T., and Smith, J.F. (2006). Stability of a practical measure of recovery from resistance training. Journal of Strength and Conditioning Research 20 (4), 756–759.

Keleman, M.H., Stewart, K.J., Gillilan, R.E., Ewart, C.K., Valenti, S.A., Manley, J.D., and Kelemen, M.D. (1986). Circuit weight training in cardiac patients. Journal of the American College of Cardiology, 7 (1), 38–42.

Kohrt, W.M., Bloomfield, S.A., Little, K.D., Nelson, M.E., and Yingling, V.R. (2004). Physical activity and bone health – position stand, American College of Sports Medicine. Medicine and Science in Sports and Exercise retrieved.

LeBlond, J., and Beals, K. ACSM Fit Society Page. (Winter 2007). Nutrition: Who needs it? If you're an athlete, you do!

Lutz, C., and Przytulski, K. (2006). Nutrition and diet therapy: Evidence-based applications. Philadelphia: F.A. Davis Company.

McArdle, W.D., Katch, F.I., and Katch, V.L. (2001). Exercise physiology: Energy, nutrition, and human performance, 5th edition. Baltimore: Lippincott, Williams & Wilkins.

MacDougall, J.D., McKelvie, R.S., Moroz, D.E., Sale, D.G., McCartney, N. and Buick, F. (1992). Factors affecting blood pressure during heavy weight lifting and static contractions. Journal of Applied Physiology, 73, 1590–1597.

Micheli, L. (1984) Pediatric and Adolescent Sports Medicine. Philadelphia: W. B. Saunders.

Misic, M.M., Valentine, R.J., Rosengren, K.S., Woods, J.A., and Evans, E.M. (2008). Impact of training modality on strength and physical function in older adults. Gerontology, 55, 411–416.

National Center for Health Statistics. (2005). Health, United States, 2005. Hyattsville, MD: U.S. Government Printing Office.

National Institute of Health. (2005). Diverticulosis and diverticulitis. http://digestive. niddk.nih.gov/ddiseases/pubs/diverticulosis/diverticulosis_508.pdf

National Institutes of Health. (2011a). Antioxidants. http://www.nlm.nih.gov/ medlineplus/antioxidants.html

National Institutes of Health. (2011b). Vitamin C. http://www.nlm.nih.gov/ medlineplus/ency/article/002404.htm

National Institutes of Health (2011c) Iron in diet. http://www.nlm.nih.gov/ medlineplus/ency/article/002422.htm

Neimann, D.C. Centers for Disease Control and Prevention. (2005). The burden of chronic diseases as causes of death, United States: National and state perspectives, 2004. www.cdc. gov/nccdphhhhp/burdenbook2004/Section01/tables

Ostchega, Y., Yoon, S.S. and Hughes, J.L. (2008). Hypertension awareness, treatment and control – continued disparities in adults: United States 2005–2006. NCHS data brief no. 3, Hyattsville, MD: National Center for Disease Statistics. 2008.

Pew Research Center (2006). Eating more, enjoying less. http://pewresearch.org/ pubs/309/eating-more-enjoying-Iess

Pollock, M.L. and Evans, W.J. (1999). Resistance training for health and disease. Medicine and Science in Sports and Exercise, 31, 10–11.

Pollock, M.L., Franklin, B.A., Balady, G.J., Chaitman, B.L., Fleg, J.L., Fletcher, B., Limacher, M., Pina, I.L., Stein, R.A., Williams, M. and Bazzarre, T. (2000). Resistance exercise in individuals with and without cardiovascular disease. Circulation 101.

Power, K., Behm, D., Cahill, F., Carroll, M., and Young, W. (2004). An acute bout of static stretching: Effects of force and jumping performance. Medicine and Science in Sports and Exercise, 36 (8), 1389–1396.

Safran, M.R. (1988). The role of warm-up in muscular injury prevention. American Journal of Sports Medicine, 16:123.

Selby, Stephen. (1997). The Archery tradition of China. www.atarn.org/Chinese/chin_ art.htm Retrieved 2/18/2013

Seguin, R and Nelson, M.E. (2003). The benefits of strength training for older adults. American Journal of Preventive Medicine, 25, 141–149.

Sheldon, W.H. and Stevens, S.S. (1942). The varieties of temperament: A psychology of constitutional differences. New York: Harper and Row Publishers.

Sigal, R.J., Kenny, G.P., Boule, N.G., Wells, G.A., Prudhomme, D., Fortier, M., Reid, R.D., Tulloch, H., Coyle, D., Phillips, P., Jennings, A. and Jaffey, J. (2007). Effects of aerobic training, resistance training, or both on glycemic control in type 2 diabetes. Annals of Internal Medicine, 147 (6) 357–369.

Sorace, P., Churilla, J.R., and Magyari, P.M. (2012). Resistance training for hypertension. American College of Sports Medicine Health and Fitness Journal, 16 (1) 13–17.

Szymanski, D.J., Szymanski, J.M., Bradford, T.J., Schade, R.L., and Pascoe, D.D. (2007). Effect of twelve weeks of medicine ball training on high school baseball players. Journal of Strength and Conditioning Research 21 (3), 654.

Tannenbaum, C. and Mayo, N. Women's health priorities and perceptions of care: A survey to identify opportunities for improving preventative health care delivery for older women. Age Ageing32: 626–635.

Thomas, K., Muir, K., Doherty, M., Jones, A., O'Reilly, S., and Bassey, E. (2002). Home based exercise programme for knee pain and knee osteoarthritis: randomized controlled trail. British Medical Journal, 325: 752.

Thompson, J., and Manore, M. (2005). Nutrition: An applied approach. San Francisco: Benjamin Cummings.

Treuth, M.S., Ryan, A.S., Pratley, R.E., Rubin, M.A., Miller, J.P., Nicklas, B.J., Sorkin, J., Harman, S.M., Goldberg, A.P., and Hurley, B.F. (1994). Effects of strength training on total and regional body composition in older men. Journal of Applied Physiology, 77 (92), 614–620.

Tzankoff, S.P. and Norris, A.H. (1977). Effect of muscle mass decrease on age-related BMR changes. Journal of Applied Physiology: Respiration and Environmental Exercise Physiology, 43 (6) 1001–1006.

United States Centers for Disease Control and Prevention and the American College of Sports Medicine. (1993). Summary statement: Workshop on physical activity and public health. Sports Medicine Bulletin, 28:7.

U.S. Department of Agriculture. ChooseMyPlate (2011). www.ChooseMyPlate.gov.

U.S. Department of Health and Human Services and U.S. Department of Agriculture. Dietary-Guidelines for Americans, 2010. 7th edition, Washington, D.C.: U.S. Government Printing Office, December 2010.

United States Department of Agriculture. Let's Eat Out: Americans Weight Taste, Convenience, and Nutrition. http://www.ers. usda.gov/publications/eib19/eib19.pdf Accessed March 3,2011.

U.S. Department of Health and Human Services. (2000). Healthy People 2010: Understanding and Improving Health. 2nd ed. Washington, D.C.: U.S. Government Printing Office, November 2000.

Wescott, W. (1996). High intensity strength training for better body composition. United States Sports Academy. Retrieved from http://www.thesportjournal.org/ article/high-intensity-strength-training-better-body-composition.

Whitney, E.N. and Rolfes, S.R. (2002). Understanding nutrition, 9th edition. Belmont, CA: Wadsworth/Thomson Learning.